Samuel Reynolds Hole

A Book About the Garden and the Gardener

Samuel Reynolds Hole

A Book About the Garden and the Gardener

ISBN/EAN: 9783337068196

Printed in Europe, USA, Canada, Australia, Japan

Cover: Foto ©Andreas Hilbeck / pixelio.de

More available books at **www.hansebooks.com**

A

BOOK ABOUT THE GARDEN

AND THE GARDENER.

BY

S. REYNOLDS HOLE,

DEAN OF ROCHESTER;

AUTHOR OF "A BOOK ABOUT ROSES," ETC.

LONDON:

EDWARD ARNOLD,

37, BEDFORD STREET, W.C.

Publisher to the India Office.

1892.

To
ALL TRUE GARDENERS
WHETHER THEY SERVE OR RULE

This Book

IS OFFERED

WITH A BROTHER'S LOVE.

PREFACE.

This book contains, with certain new additions, *The Six of Spades* and other articles, which were written long ago (with the exception of *The Joy of a Garden*, which appeared in the London *Guardian* some twelve months ago), and were received by the public and by the press with much sympathy and kind approbation. They were written, and are republished, from an earnest desire to enlarge that love of a garden, which brings so much pure enjoyment to the gardener, whatever may be his position in life. Whether he reside in a castle or a cottage, it makes his home more dear to him, and helps him, by satisfaction ever new, "therewith to be content." When the author pleads that children at home, boys at school, young men at college, villagers, and citizens, should have every encouragement and opportunity for appreciating the beauty of things pleasant to the eye, and the utility of things good for food, he writes from practical results, and not from theories. For example, it was my custom for many summers to take walks by the brookside, and in the fields and woods, on Sunday evening, with the children of the school, as I have recorded at page 88. Twenty years after, I had some hours to wait for a train at a great Yorkshire station, and recognized in one of the porters a schoolboy, who had often joined in our floral promenades. He invited me to visit his home, and when we reached a long row of houses, exactly alike in size and structure, he stopped and asked: "Now, sir, can you tell me which of these houses is mine?" I looked, and answered as I looked, "Yes, Joe, *that* is your home with the little flower-beds in front, and the climbing plant on the wall." And I remember the smile on his face (the smile, and something more), as he said, "I have never forgotten those Sunday walks. I have never lost my love of the Flowers."

The same happy experience has come to me from efforts to promote among our poorer brethren the gratification and the benefits of a Garden (see page 177), and no man rejoices more than I do in the present efforts of our statesmen to extend the Allotment System. They will meet with two opponents. Idle men won't have gardens, and ignorant men won't know how to use them. If politicians would send teachers of horticulture into our villages, and would show the men how to grow fruit and vegetables, and the women how to preserve and cook them, I should have some faith in their "Reforms."

S. R. H.

The Deanery, Rochester,
March, 1892.

CONTENTS.

	PAGE
THE GARDENER'S DREAM	1
THE JOY OF A GARDEN	18
THE SIX OF SPADES—	
I. Mr. Oldacre	29
II. Mr. Chiswick	37
III. Mr. Evans	47
IV. Mr. Grundy	58
V. The Curate	75
VI. The Club in Session	93
VII. The President's Lecture—"Rosa Bonheur"	98
VIII. Mr. Oldacre's Story—The Lady Alice	119
IX. Mr. Chiswick on Bedding-out	138
X. Mr. Evans on Shows and Showing	167
XI. Mr. Grundy's Song	188
XII. My Miniature Garden	192
MY FIRST FIGHT IN THE WARS OF THE ROSES	202
SOME CORNISH GARDENS	216
THE SPRING GARDEN AT BELVOIR	231

CONTENTS.

	PAGE
Alpine Gardens	237
The Carnation	241
A Wall of Flowers	249
Types of Gardeners	250
The Song of the Exhibitor	255
"Love Among the Tea Roses" (*and Frontispiece*)	257

A BOOK ABOUT THE GARDEN AND THE GARDENER.

THE GARDENER'S DREAM.

I had attached myself one evening to the slimmer end of a big Broseley pipe, and my mind in musing about many things,

"Tenui meditamur avena,"

settled finally, like a weary butterfly upon a Rose, on the recreations and amusements of life. And when I asked myself which of them all brings the longer and larger happiness, there appeared amid the smoke a medium of communication so frequently adopted by our old friends the Genii in the "Arabian Nights," the vision of a man. A bright, pleasant, healthful face smiled beneath a cap of glossy velvet; two diamond eyes shone in the head of a golden fox, which fastened the folds of a snowy neckerchief, white and smooth as the petal of a Camellia; a coat of scarlet, glowing like a Poinsettia, was buttoned over a blue bird's-eye vest; and warm, easy, well-fitting, thick-ribbed "cords" disappeared into a pair of pale brown "tops." "There never, my boy," he gaily observed, "can be the faintest whimper of a doubt that the greatest fun in all the world is the fun of riding to hounds. To leave a discomfited host of skirters and craners, drawn up aghast at a scowling stile, or galloping ruefully by some chilly stream in search of ford or bridge; and then pressing on pasture, and pulling in plough, to have forty minutes, and 'who-op' in the open! By Jove, old fellow" (and here he fenced at my ribs with his hunting-whip),

"Kings it makes gods, and meaner creatures kings."

And I made answer to this festive phantom in breeches, and I said, "True, crimson spectre, true. Hunting is undoubtedly of sports the Pope, but, alas! not more infallible. It happens to its keenest sons sometimes to be yearning for a start at one particular corner of a gorse, just when the fox goes away best pace in a precisely opposite direction; and then, oh, brother of the gamboge boots, the riding after hounds is vanity. And the wind of horses is an uncertain thing; and the stub, and over-reach, and pointed stake are perils great and hateful; and banks are treacherous and ditches blind, and there is ever a maniac on a rushing chestnut, to jump upon us when we fall; and clays are succulent, and many black-smiths fools, and it saddens a horseman's heart to hear, 'Mr. Jones, sir, you've lost a shoe;' and the dogs of shepherds are accursed things; and bird-tenters, holloaing as though they saw the fox, are men unfit to live: and—yes, I see your derisive smile, and I quite agree that hunting is, despite these drawbacks, the cheeriest pastime and the bravest exercise that stirs the sportsman's heart; but after all, sweet vision of the speckled vest, it lasts but four months of the year, and much of this time may be lost and null, being 'sullied by a frost;' and tell me, what shall mournful hunters do when lambs are bleating for their mas, 'and the green leaves come again'?"

Then the hunting-cap changed into a soft "billy-cock," and the pink, and the cords, and the tops into a Norfolk jacket, and knickerbockers, and ankle boots; and another apparition, stalwart and ruddy as the first, stood, with a breech-loader on his broad shoulder, and said, "Let me suggest the gun: think of the pure, bracing, moorland air; of the grouse, rising with a whir and with a crow, and then tumbling with a thud among the heather; of the dinner and the rubber in our cosy shooting lodge; of the weed and the whiskey, 'as ye tell how they fell.' Think, oh think of the grand excitement of deer-stalking! the first distant sight of some glorious stag, the antlered monarch of the waste; of the long, the subtle, the laborious stalk, when brain and body, mind and muscle seem to glow like the wheels of swift machinery, and to gain from the grand excitement of the hour a strange, victorious energy; and then the crisis, the awful ecstasy, when the rifle is raised, and the stricken deer takes his last wild leap, and falls with a crash to die. Think, too, of quiet, pleasant days with genial friends in bright sunny September; of truthful 'Don,' stanch upon his point, and 'Belle' backing him, sixty yards off; of the panniered pony with the welcome lunch, and the laughing girls who spread it for us beneath the brave old oak. Recall those frosty mornings in December, quickening the blood and sharpening the wits, and the cheery congress of shooters, keepers, beaters, and retrievers, forming into line along the grassy 'riding.' Listen again to the nimble sticks, clattering amid the trees, gaily as the shillelaghs in an Irish row, and ever and anon beating a wild tattoo, with an accompaniment of yells, hardly to be surpassed by betting-men, or any other lunatics, and called forth by an ambition, ever fruitless, to 'stop that rabbit back.' Hearken once more, for there is a cry of still intenser interest: a voice as full of deep emotion as if the owner had roused a buffalo, or flushed his uncle's ghost, is heard to shriek, 'Mark woodcock! and we bring him down, as he glides into the open, to the immense disgust of Smith, outside the covert, who has just raised his gun to fire. Think, finally, of wild ducks, quacking out of sedgy streams, and of glad retrievers springing from the bank, and shaking the water from their glossy curls, as they lay the mallard at your feet!"

And I said, "Oh, Knickerbockers, thy words are true, but they tell not all the truth. Thou hast been reticent with reference to mournful hours, when the lordly stag was startled by thy rifle, a moment sniffed the tainted gale, and then trotted quietly away unhurt, disdainful, as the gillies winking near, and the deerhound growling at thy side. Thou hast said nothing of other feverish and fretful days, when, owing to 'that confounded old Madeira,' or 'that weed of Green's,' or that fixed determination to take the conceit from out of that bumptious Brown, thou didst 'never shoot so infamously,' and thy gun seemed to be under a fiendish power, and would not bear upon the game. Reserve has padlocked thy sweet lips, my friend, and memory lost the key, as regards a certain other woodcock, which, twice spared by thy mercy, fell stone dead for Brown—Brown, the vainglorious—Brown, the hateful, who last night flirted with thy lady love, and will to-night proclaim to a large assembly how splendidly he wiped thine eye. Thou art oblivious, moreover, of mornings wretched, when thou camest home to breakfast, blue with cold and black with disappointment, and the great retriever had snarled significantly, eying thy gaitered calves. And thou hast not forgotten to forget those chilly nights, when 'flight time' found thee shivering like the willow above thee; and the ducks had a prior engagement. Thou hast not been garrulous how poachers poach; how foxes (not that I love them less) abduct the sitting partridge, and mowers slice them with the ruthless scythe; how chough and crow, and chattering pies and jays feast on the pheasant's egg; how weasels drink, like Freshmen wine, the dying coney's blood. 'Silent, oh Moyle,' hast thou been on pointers, chasing recklessly the flying leveret, and barking as though they sang to their keepers, 'Whistle, and I'll come to thee, my love,' when I've put up all the game. And yet as the old lady, improving Cowper, was kind enough to say of her country—

'England, with all thy faults, I cannot help loving thee still;

so, *malgre defauts*, I rejoice with you in dog and gun. Shooting (I exclude, of course, the unmanly massacre of tame pheasants, driven into a corner and there shot down, ten yards from a dozen breech-loaders, amid a villainous stench of saltpetre)—shooting is one of those exercises which make Englishmen quick and capable of work above more sedentary folk; but I am inquiring now for some recreation of a more sure and a more lasting quality, one which may reasonably refresh body and mind, not only in the autumn and winter, but in the spring and summer of the year."

As the word "summer" passed my lips "a change came o'er the spirit of my dream." I stood by a broad river, now flowing in such lucid transparency over its shallows, that every pebble polished bright was seen distinct and clear, the large stones rising above the stream, half wet, half dry, like those timid bathers who dread their primal plunge, and now deepening into darker pools, where the swift waters seemed to rest and pause, on their journey to distant seas. And I was admiring the trees, which came down the sloping banks, as it were, to see their loveliness in that shining mirror, and the great mountains far away beyond, when a shout of jubilation drew my gaze to a gentleman, in ecstasies and a Tweed suit, who stood, or, more truthfully speaking, capered, upon the opposite bank. He pointed to a magnificent salmon, its silvery scales shimmering in the sunlight (this beautiful example of Sigmatismus is entered at Stationers' Hall, and to imitate it much is felony)—such a one as you have seen at Mr. Grove's, in Bond Street, and weighing over 30lbs. He roared across the river Kingsley's line,

"Was ever salmon yet that shone so fair?"

together with an invitation to dine; and in two seconds, as ever in dreams, we had dined excellently, and I was sitting in his snuggery, an apartment adorned with rods, and nets, and gaffs: with fishing boots, which he called his "Wade-Mecums;" with a small library of books, all filled with fly-leaves; with boxes of feathers, fluffs, and furs; and having, over the mantel-piece, the usual perch, enormous, with his eyes half out of his head, from surprise at his own obesity.

Forthwith he commenced an elaborate dissertation on the life of a complete angler. It was a life, he said, of calm contentment, and of a sweet and thankful peace. It was passed amid scenes of surpassing beauty, the wild grandeur of Connemara's mountains, the solemn stillness of Norwegian fiords, the cheerful loveliness of Scotland's lakes, the sunny song-fraught charms of England's meadow-streams. To enhance, at intervals, these simple joys, there were such excitements as I had seen that day—the giant fish, fast hooked and fighting for his life, now shooting away like a rocket, now flinging himself in noble rage above the stream, now dropping, plumb and ponderous, down—testing in every way, not only hook, and line, and rod, but human pluck and skill—at last defeated, gaffed, and brought ashore! Then spake he glowing words of trout and grayling, perch and monstrous pike. He showed me flies, which the oldest, wiliest, most abstemious fish could not find in his heart to pass, rushing blindly to his mournful doom, just as one sees some ancient bachelor go mad for Miss in her teens. For several he had special names. That was "The Barmaid" sure to charm the topers of the deep; this was "Syren;" there "Bonne-bouche;" and here was "Look-and-Die." He gazed as fondly on his Limerick hooks as though they were Irish eyes. Then he showed me knots which were never loosened, and nooses which were ever free. He taught me how to gather and throw the castnet; and I, his pupil apt, caught—my first cast—his lamp, cigars, and whiskey. Finally he adjured me, by his rods, to fish—fish always, and be blessed.

"O Pescatore," I answered sweetly, "in this alone our hearts conspire, that if I do, I'm blest. Your line is not mine, O friend. My angle has been obtuse, my fishing common plaice, from my youth. I shall never be a judicious Hooker. I get entangled in the branches of trees, my kingfisher; I bring ashore decaying sticks, and long, green, trailing weeds. And when, at last, the long-sought crisis comes, and the float, supine and motionless so many dreary hours, awakes to active life: and my happy heart beats in unison, pit-a-pat, with its rise and fall, until down it goes, disappearing in the deep; and I give him time, 'to make assurance surer,' and finally strike and bring out my prey; it is always the old eternal snig, which, but a size larger than the bait itself, not only contrives to gorge it wholly, but to fix it by some disgusting process in the centre of its slimy form. I can bear no more. Dissolve, vision. Vanish, gentle Angler, Go!"

The Angler vanished, and was followed by a succession of tableaux vivants, representations of our sports, pastimes, and recreations. The gentleman rider, pale from training, and excitement too, but cool and brave as Curtius, came down at speed to the broad, sullen water, and cleared it, while a thousand cheered. The gentleman "whip" sat upon his dark handsome drag, driving with a quiet and graceful ease his high-bred four-in-hand. Cricketers, rejoicing in youth and health, lithe of limb and springy as deer, made magnificent hits to square leg for six, and ran with the speed of Fortunio's Lightfoot to achieve the distant catch. The yachtsman, all sails set, steered past the winning buoy, and great guns boomed his victory. The oarsman pulled his long, steady stroke, and his eye flashed with a righteous pride, as the men of his university, or the boys of his school, were shouting his well-won praise. The tennis-player stood, racket in hand, watching the ball as it came bounding from "the service-side," foreseeing all its varied course, calmly waiting its final fall, sending it like a bullet into the Dedans (friends will be pleased to accept this intimation, and to duck their heads if they want their eyesight), and so winning the set. Archers, with yew bows, and archeresses, with beaux yeux, were filled with the "sacra auri fames," and yearned to hit the gold. The billiard-player, a little over-perfumed by stale tobacco and gas, but with a marvellous eyesight and power of cue, screwed in from spot, and played from a half-a-dozen cushions, or with "no end of side," his clever cannon-game. The skater glided on the frozen lake, at ease and happy on a single leg, as the still heron on its distant shore. Bowls slowly travelled towards the "jack" along the level sward, while solemn faces, smoking long pipes of clay, watched the insipid, though once royal game. Croquet-players, with smiles too thin to veil the scowls beneath, and with tones which said, "I assure you, darling," but which meant, "Oh, you horrid cheat!" placed lovely boots upon the boxwood ball, and routed the flying foe. Skittles fell with a dull, rumbling sound; quoits rang upon the iron "hob;" single-sticks resounded like the brattling horns of deer; and every sport, amusement, recreation, game, went on in full force before me.

Not one of them fulfilled my heart's desire; and yet I was interested in them all (barring the bowls), experienced in most, and expert in some. Horses have I loved fondly ever since a subtle groom slipped noiselessly from his seat behind me: and, fear giving away to pride, I cantered in alone to my applauding friends, as Gladiateur won the Derby. Guns I have held since, a mere child, I stole away to neighbouring corn-fields, making friends with a youthful "bird-tenter," who loaded a long single barrel with the bowl of a broken pipe, and who taught me, after many twitchings and blinkings, to bring down the sedentary "spink." All English sports and games I have loved and love, and yet they satisfied not my present need. "Give me," I cried, "something more continuous than these—something which may occupy the thoughts, and employ the actions of my leisure, not in summer only, as cricket, not in winter only, as the chase, but alike in every season of the year; and, more than this, through all the different phases of my life—youth, manhood, and old age."

Whereupon, and as in a dissolving view, the whole scene faded from my sight, and in its place appeared before me another semblance of a man. He wore a loose picturesque costume of velvet, and had a pleasant, handsome, intellectual presence, despite a superfluity of hair, which showed that the proprietor was not enrolled in Mr. Truefitt's "Toilette Club." "Essay," he said, "some nobler exercise, worthier the mind of man. Try painting—try 'the art which baffles Time's tyrannic sway,' which lives exultingly in a glorious world of its own, which, lodging in an attic, and looking out on a London fog, can surround itself with the magnificence of a palace, and the scenery of an Italian lake. Or try music—music, which evokes the heroism, exalts the piety, and soothes the sorrows of mankind."

"Alas!" I replied, "I have tried and failed: and you might as well essay to teach a boot-jack chemistry, or listen for a symphony from your garden roller, as tell a man to be an artist. Art is not precisely what the old lady thought it was, when she asked the son of Canova 'whether he meant to carry on his father's business?' It is indigenous to the soil in which it grows, and there only can it be seen in its perfection. You may transplant, and by incessant care you may obtain a similitude; but there will ever be the same sad difference which exists between two plants of Coleus—the one in a stove, the other in a cold clay soil; or between the golden eagle rising from his aerie, like a king from his throne, with a solemn grace and beauty, and the same bird, heart-broken, diseased, and draggled in a cage. No, friend, earnestly as I admire and love the arts, I am not to be an artist. When I had progressed as far as 'Home, sweet home' on the flute, I felt I had climbed my height; and as a painter my career was stayed by incapacity, stubborn and chronic, to prevent the distant objects of my landscape from advancing boldly in a line and occupying the entire foreground." He favoured me with a smile, half pity, half disgust, as though I were one of those unhappy cripples whom one meets sometimes, strapped to a board upon castors, and propelling themselves along our pavements; and then he was gone.

Then came, last scene of all to end this strange, and to me eventful history, the final ghost: and I felt a presentiment, nay, a conviction, as he took the chair opposite to mine, and filled the large white bowl of his pipe, that he possessed the power to dispel my doubts, and to reveal the object for which my spirit yearned. He gave me that assuring smile which one sometimes sees upon a partner's face, when, wanting the odd trick to win a rubber, and having realized six he holds the last trump card in his hand. The smile lit up a face, which you could not mistrust, frank and truthful, "fresh as English air could make it," and bright with the afterglow of sixty summers. He was tall, erect, and active, and though Time's snow lay on his broad brow, his winter days were those of a merry Christmas, when the air is pure and bracing, and the heart full of love and hope. He took a few preliminary puffs to test the quality of my tobacco, and then addressed me thus:—

"You probably possess among your paternal pictures the portrait of a gentleman, looking for his spectacles, with the object of his search on the top of his forehead; at all events, you are his true kinsman, and the family likeness is very interesting. Permit me to suggest an addition to the gallery—yourself with a brace of greyhounds, the trio gazing, heads up, over distant fields, while a hare squats close to your feet. You should read the story, one of the most charming ever told, of the French gentleman who came home one day in a melancholy, discontented mood, envying his rich neighbour, whom he had just left, starting for a tour in an elegant equipage, with courier and valet, and every luxury, and complaining bitterly of his own scanty means, which kept him a wretched prisoner at home, like a donkey tethered on a common. In this unmanly and unthankful temper, his eye happened to turn towards the western heavens, and there he saw that wondrous spectacle of beauty, the sun going down in glory. Awed by that sublime splendour, the dark spirit of evil fled, as from Saul, when David took a harp and played with his hand; and gratitude and sweet content returned with the thought that not in the whole world could traveller find a lovelier scene than this. The sun set upon a wiser and a happier man. Henceforth his eyes, and ears, and heart were opened, to see, not only such scenes of grandeur as that which had just passed away, but traces of a divine beauty in the minutest works around him; to hear 'the manifold soft chimes' of bird, and breeze, and stream; to love them one and all. The next morning Monsieur Alphonse Karr began that 'Tour round my Garden,' which I now urge you first to read, and then to realize.

"You call yourself a gardener, and a florist, but if you were so, earnestly and thoroughly, you would not be now inquiring what recreation brings to man the longer and larger happiness. You would have known ere this that 'gardening,' as Lord Bacon tells us, 'is the purest of human pleasures, the greatest refreshment to the spirit of man,' and that 'the life and felicity of an excellent gardener is,' as truly now as when Evelyn wrote, 'to be preferred before all other diversions.' Hear evidence which you cannot dispute, but must sign seal and deliver, as your own act and deed. This very day, in the most dismal month of our English year—

> 'No sun, no moon,
> No morn, no noon,
> No——vember,'

you have had your chief enjoyment from your garden. After breakfast you went into your rosary, and you cut a bouquet from Gloire de Dijon, Madame Masson, Jules Margottin, Madame Domage, Senateur Vaisse, and Souvenir de la Malmaison; which, placed on your writing table, brightened your room throughout the day. Tired with a long correspondence and other business, you refreshed your spirit with a survey of your little greenhouse, gay with Chrysanthemums, with those Hybrid Pelargoniums, which recall so pleasantly dear, quaint, old Donald Beaton, with Epacris, Primula, and Fuchsia, and sweet with Violets, Mignonette, Genista, and Heliotrope. At luncheon you feasted on the half of a Marechal de la Cour Pear, whose growth you had watched for weeks, and which weighed 18oz. when it fell. In the afternoon you opened, with the keen, glad interest which a schoolboy feels when he cuts the string of his hamper from home, a bundle of new Rose-trees from one of the great nurseries, disposed them in your rosarium, and helped to plant. Then you superintended the arrangement of your small winter garden, the Thujas, Aucubas, Gold and Silver Hollies, Arabis, Ivies, and Heaths, which you keep in pots for the purpose, and which are to 'cheer the ungenial day,' until the Snowdrop and Crocus, the Tulip and the Hyacinth, proclaim, as heralds, another festival of flowers. Then, having looked into your fruit-room, and counted, like a miser, your golden store; having glanced with a paternal pride over your numerous progeny of 'nursery' stock, the rising generation of dandies and belles, who are to rule the beau-monde next year, you went into your vinery, and cut those grand bunches of Muscats and Hamburghs, which not only made you a dessert fit for an emperor, but, taken in part to a sick neighbour, brought you a far greater luxury—'the luxury of doing good.'

"And so it is, that every day brings to a gardener its special interests. There is always something worthy of his care and admiration, some new development of beauty, some fresh design to execute, some lesson to learn, some genial work to do. Stormy days, which mar the sportsman's hopes, affect him not. In his stove, gay now with Achimines, Dracænas, Crotons, Ardisias, Begonias, Ipomœas, Amaryllis, and with many a lovely Fern and Lycopod, he finds perpetual summer; in his orchard-house and in his conservatory, perpetual spring. And not only is the gardener's happiness thus in its duration sure, but it is in its peculiar essence of a very sweet and gracious quality. It ministers health to the body, and it ministers health to the mind. It brings pure air to the lungs, and pure, reverent thoughts to the heart. It makes us love our home, content and satisfied with those true pleasures which neither sting nor pall; and yet, when we leave that home, it follows us wheresoever we go. As

> 'All places, which the eye of Heaven visits,
> Are to a wise man ports and happy havens,'

so in all gardens, and in all gardeners, we find a home and brothers. There is always a welcome, always a sympathy. In horticulture there is less rivalry, less jealousy, than in other enterprises, because, first of all, the very practice of it tends to make men generous and wise, and because the arena is so large, and the spheres of excellence so numerous, that none need interfere with his neighbour, or insist on riding his hobby. I can thoroughly enjoy White's Orchids and Black's Pinetum, Brown's Orchard House, and Green's Fernery. They in turn rejoice in my Roses. I do not say that there are no envyings and no disappointments, but that these are fewer in horticulture than in any other recreation; and it is so, because 'Nature never did betray the heart that loved her,' never failed to instruct the humble student of her wisdom, nor refused to smile upon the fond admirers of her beauty."

I looked up to express my consent and penitence, but my ghostly adviser was gone. I awoke from my dream, and from my doubts. My eyes were opened from a darker blindness than sleep, and I learned to verify in the happiness of a life the lessons of my Gardener's Dream.

THE JOY OF A GARDEN.

To appreciate the supreme happiness of a garden you must first be ill. Any malady will do—influenza, ancient or modern, measles, rheumatism, whooping cough, or gout, which keeps you ten days in bed, and causes you to moan and groan. You must be familiar with those dolorous expressions of restlessness and discomfort, *quas Natura suâ sponte suggerit* (as we read in our Oxford logic) which nature suggests for your relief, when settling yourself on your left side for a long, refreshing sleep, you find, after two minutes, that the position is untenable, and change it only to encounter a similar disappointment. You must have known what it is to recede with abhorrence from the "lovely sweet-bread," the "delicious whiting," the "charming cutlet," so carefully prepared, so fondly proffered, and you must still be haunted with dim memories of a procession which seemed to be always parading your apartment, smiling Hebes, bearing cups of "Liebig's Extract," "Brand's Essence," arrowroot, jellies, and barleywater. Nor have you forgotten that dreadful dream, in which, your temperature having transcended your normal heat, you found yourself in the scanty raiment of the night, and only a small red flag in your hand, in the middle of the bull-ring at Madrid, the centre of attraction to a countless multitude of spectators, and a special object of interest to a huge red bull, preparing with a preliminary whisk of his tail to charge down upon you.

At last "a change comes o'er the spirit of this dream." "Things at the worst will cease, or else climb upward, to which they were before." You retire from the perilous vocation of a matador into the serenities of private life. There are signs of returning health. Your food resumes its ancient flavour. The odour of your mutton chop "nimbly and sweetly recommends itself unto your outer senses;" and, when no one is looking, you gnaw the bone. You discover merit in viands hitherto unknown or disdained—tapioca, sago, rice ground and sloppy. The batter-pudding takes you back to the nursery, and to that nurse who was so mean with the sugar, and the pancakes recall those jubilant Shrove Tuesdays in the servants' hall, when your small fingers dropped the brass, numbered, ball into the wooden pillar, and "raffling for oranges" was not forbidden by the law. The fantastic figures and weird faces, which you have watched in the flickering firelight, disappear from curtain and screen, and that enormous bird which, with a terrible beak and a sinister eye, has been gazing at you, as the vulture gazed on Prometheus, wears quite a benevolent look.

"*Cras ingens iterabimus aequor*"—"to-morrow you may go downstairs." You make a feeble joke (excused in consideration of your debility) that you will be no longer the prisoner with a Chill-on; and next day, languidly, lacking the vigour and elasticity of the march of the Cameron men, with a gait suggestive to an ill-informed suspicion rather of alcohol than of toast and water, with an incomplete smile upon your countenance as you meet some member of your household, you descend to an easy chair, which is set for you by a glowing fire (though it is the last day in May), and once more with a thankful heart survey the books, the pictures, and all the beloved surroundings of your study. How clean and bright and orderly the old workshop looks; but you are not to work. There are piles of parcels, and envelopes of all denominations, on a table near, and these you are permitted to open, leisurely, casting with a savage disdain your rejected addresses, invitations to take tickets in lotteries, to borrow money, to invest in mines, to poison yourself with golden sherries, tawny ports, creamy champagnes, chiefly manufactured in London, to secure yourself from all the ills which flesh is heir to by taking syrups and pills, which are warranted to make old men young —tearing these tentative frauds into fragments and flinging them into the capacious basket at your feet, which seems to say, without words, "Rubbish may be shot here."

"Shapeless idleness!" Is *dolce far niente* ever

true to men who realize the dignity of manhood and know that work is happiness—

> " 'Tis the primal curse,
> But softened into mercy, made the spring
> Of cheerful days, and nights without a groan ? "

Oh yes, to the weary and the weak—welcome as the halt and the dispersal to the soldier footsore from the long, hot, dusty march, or as the "easy all" to the oarsman, when "forty strokes a minute is the pace we go." Idleness, like fire, is a splendid servant, but a cruel master. Idleness to labour overstrained is the fallow which comes after the plough in autumn. Idleness to the idle is the rank growth on neglected land of worthless tares and weeds, whereof the mower filleth not his hand, nor he that bindeth up the sheaves his bosom :—

> " An unweeded garden
> That grows to seed : things rank and gross in Nature
> Possess it merely."

Compensation and retribution are ever manifest in the results of industry and sloth. The sleep of a labouring man is sweet whether he eat little or much, but the abundance of the rich will not suffer him to sleep :—

> " Weariness
> Can snore upon the flint, while resty sloth
> Finds the down pillow hard."

" I was a happier man," it was said by one of our merchant princes, " when I was hard at work as a poor clerk in Liverpool than I am now with my grand houses, and gardens, and servants, and equipages, half-a-million of money, and *nothing to do.*"

No restoration so sure as this honest rest, and accordingly when you have been two or three days "downstairs" your benign physician comes to you on a sunny afternoon, opens your prison door, and allows you half-an-hour in your garden. So fresh, so sweet, so beautiful, that you feel like Linnæus when he saw for the first time an English common, all aglow with golden gorse, or like Longfellow, when he stood on the bridge at midnight, and a flood of thoughts came gushing, and filled his eyes with tears. The rooks seem to caw congratulations, and a mellow ouzel, fluting in the elm, to welcome with musical honours. Some lovely visitors are gone. The last roseate blossoms have floated from the almond tree, that gracious harbinger, which sets the first and fairest smile of spring, not only on our country, but on our city and suburban gardens. Forsythia suspensa, pronounced by one of our most reliable authorities, Mr. W. Robinson, in his "English Flower-garden," to be "the most charming hardy deciduous shrub we possess," has lost its golden bells. Pyrus malus floribunda, another gem of purest ray serene in Flora's vernal coronet—no gardener forgets his glad surprise, when he first saw it completely covered with its white pink and red efflorescence, how he murmured mentally "*must* have that," made a memorandum, wrote to his nurseryman—has put off its gay garments, and now, in workday dress, is forming its tiny fruit, miniature apples, perfect in form, about the dimensions of a pill, and making the most delectable dish for a Lord Mayor's banquet in Liliput, or a doll's dessert at home. Another pyrus, from the same country, japonica, but of a very different order, is also engaged in transforming its large, glowing flowers into fruit, into pears, which I had never seen upon it until I left the shires. The snow has disappeared from the mespilus (*praetereunt nives*), and the medlars, which follow, few and feeble, do not console us, as with its neighbour, prunus pisardi, which, when its bloom is gone, still fascinates, when the sun shines, with the deep red glow of its leaves. Some others of the flowering trees and shrubs, wild cherries, and crabs, the daphne mezereon, have faded and gone; but as when fair maids of honour have fulfilled their court-service and left the castle, other winsome ladies-in-waiting maintain their dignity and grace, so now in our English gardens, from the primrose to the Christmas-rose, from the first daffodil to the last dahlia, we have a continuous succession of beauty. There are some of us who can recall with bitterness and shame a time when this was not so; when it could no longer be said—

"The daughters of the year,
One after one, through that still garden past,
Each garlanded with her peculiar flower,
Danced into light and died into the shade;
And each in passing touched with some new grace."

There was a Reign of Terror, though we, who reigned, were triumphant rather than terrified in our fools' paradise. We went about like—very like—

executioners with our axes hacking at trees on which
we ought to have been hanged, and shedding their
innocent sap over the land. We grubbed, and
stubbed, and made bonfires, and all but danced,
like wild Indians, around the wooden tenements
which the white men had built for their abode.
Were we not assured that our floral forefathers, of
course with the most amiable intentions and delightful sentiments, knew nothing whatever of horticulture, and that it had been reserved for us to reveal to
an astonished world the true grandeur and glory of a
garden? Wherefore we cleared away beds and borders,
turfing and levelling, and then with measuring tape
and iron skewers, and other instruments of torture,
we traced our great geometrical design of circles and
semicircles, quadrangles and triangles, rhomboids
and parallelograms, stars, tadpoles, and snakes. And
now, let cannons roar their *feu de joie*, as on the
coronation of a king! let bells peal forth from every
tower, "ring out the old, ring in the new!" let huge
trombones and monster drums declare the advent of
"the conquering hero!" for the time of "bedding-
out" is here, and the royal procession comes on—in
wheelbarrows!—right Royal, nevertheless, in scarlet
and gold (pelargonium and calceolaria), Imperial,
Episcopal, in purple (verbena), accompanied by their
attendants, wearing, in flower or in leaf, all other
hues, the darkest, by perilla, almost black, and coleus
—the lightest by centauria and cineraria maritima,
blue by lobelia, grey by dwarf ageratum, shades of
yellow by pansies, gazanias, and tagetes, rose and
pink by verbenas and pelargoniums. Added to these,

and perhaps the most reliable of all for prettiness and endurance, the geranium, with variegated foliage, such as Bijou and Flower of Spring with *silver*, Golden Chain and Crystal Palace with *golden* edgings.

It cannot be denied—penitent as we are, we have no wish to deny—that this sudden splendour, when the specimens had been cultured with care and arranged with taste as to size and colour, was universally admired. The novel and brilliant appearance of large groups of plants out-of-doors, which had hitherto been only seen singly in pots under glass, brought a new sensation to all sorts and conditions of men and women. Grand old gardeners and ancient foresters expressed their delight and astonishment. Emotional young ladies pronounced it to be "quite too utter," and even undergraduates, who consider it bad form to express their feelings, except at a boat-race or in the Sheldonian Theatre, were constrained to admit that it was "rather jolly." Then arose emulation and strife. The squire's gardener had 10,000, the baronet's 20,000, the earl's 30,000, and the duke's 50,000 plants.

Time went on; our enthusiasm went off. First of all we began to miss some of those sweet old friends of our childhood whom we had so cruelly expelled; nor did the sight of their successors in thumb pots, on shelves, under stages, in vineries and frame, console us. Then we began to complain that the time was long and tedious before our new friends, which could not be brought *al fresco* until the end of May, came into full growth and bloom; and even when the display was gayest and brightest we discovered that we were quickly satisfied by brief and infrequent surveys. And then, on the eve of our garden party, to which we had invited the *élite* of the county, joyfully hoping to plunge most of them into the depths of an envious despair, *that storm!* early in July, a thunderstorm, a hailstorm, and lo! my grand picture looked more like a palette; the brightness and the colour and the form were gone from the drenched and drooping flowers, and melancholy marked me for her own. Like Cowper, patriot and poet, I loved England still, "though," as on several previous occasions, "deformed by sullen rains;" but I was no longer enamoured of that portion of my country which is allotted to "bedding-out."

So I became a sadder and a wiser gardener. I meekly confessed, "Great nature is more wise than I," and felt heartily ashamed of my disparagements of my floral ancestors, recalling painfully one of their trite aphorisms, "Young men *think* that old men are fools, but old men *know* that young men are foolish." I made new beds, I enlarged my borders, and, only a year after that fatal storm, young men and maidens were playing tennis on the scene of the disaster. The exiles were recalled, and the natural, the English, system of gardening, which gives us something to admire in ten months out of the twelve, once more—

"With nobler grace
Diffused its artless beauties o'er the place."

These henceforth absorbed my allegiance and

admiration. Never more happily than now (hence this long divergence), as I come forth from my doleful captivity and see, in place of the fair visitors whom I have named, the Wistaria Sinesis, with its long, graceful racemes of pale purple flowers, the pink and scarlet Thorns, the Laburnum, with its golden fountains, the Syringas, lilac and white, Marie Lemoine and Charles X., the lovely Weigelas, Darwin's bright yellow Barberis, *toujours gai*, the white Horse Chestnut, admirably contrasting with its neighbour a copper beech, blonde and brunette, Minnie and Brenda, and its sister, inviting a like comparison between its roseate blossoms and the silvery leafage of Acer negundo variegatum.

So with the flowers and plants, as with the trees and shrubs. The aconites, snowdrops, crocuses, and hyacinths have disappeared; a solitary scarlet tulip glows in the border like a soldier in a crowd at a cricket match; the narcissus—how gloriously they have represented their noble names, Emperor and Empress (queen of them all), Maximus, and Grandis, Incomparabilis, Poeticus (Shakespeare, Herrick, and Keats have been their Laureates)—the daffodils droop to die; the primulas and polyanthus gladden our eyes no more with their infinite variety. But what an abundance of beauty succeeds! That group of iris (germanica) and doronicum reminds us of the cohorts of the Assyrians, "all gleaming with purple and gold." How prettily the pansies and anemones are clustering round the great clumps of delphinium, and pyrethrum, and lupin, and pæony! But we have lingered too long *in limine* for this general survey from the garden door. Let us move on for a more minute inspection of those gracious gifts which bring to us in the joy of a garden "the purest of human pleasures, and the greatest refreshment to the spirit of man."

THE SIX OF SPADES.

CHAPTER I.

MR. OLDACRE.

My Lord Dufferin, in his "Letters from High Latitudes," tells the affecting story of a conscientious cock, who, perplexed by the perpetual sunshine, and unable to discharge the vocal duties which seemed to ensue therefrom, eventually crowed himself mad, and put an end to his existence with his own wings, by abruptly flying into the sea. "As we proceeded north," he writes, "and the nights became shorter, the cock we had shipped at Stornoway became quite bewildered on the subject of that meteorological phenomenon, the dawn of day. In fact, I doubt whether he ever slept for more than five minutes at a stretch, without waking up in a state of nervous excitement lest it should be cockcrow. At last, when night ceased altogether, his constitution could no longer stand the shock. He crowed once or twice sarcastically; then went melancholy mad; finally, taking a calenture, he cackled lowly (probably of green fields), and leaping overboard, drowned himself!"

It is, I say, a sorrowful story, especially when we reflect that under happier circumstances this cock might have reached a good old age, and seen his daughters laying peacefully around him, and his sons a-fighting one another like anything.

Analogously, I go on to consider whatever would become of us gardeners and florists if we were sentenced to an everlasting summer—if our conservatories within, and our gardens without, were, day after day, and week upon week, to glow with undiminished splendour, and make the air heavy with exhaustless odours. Would not our eyes be dazzled into weariness, aching and winking, as when in our early youth we overdid them with our new kaleidoscope? Would not our nostrils finally be enforced to entreat the intervention of our forefingers and thumbs, to supplicate the presence of our pocket-handkerchief, lest we should die of aromatic pain?

Our powers of appreciating the beautiful are finite, soon tire, and need repose. What appetites we bring home from the loveliest scenery! How thirsty we were at Tintern! What a luncheon we made at the Trossachs hotel! How we rush from the pre-Raphaelite glories of the exhibition to our strawberries and iced cream at Grange's! How palatable the oysters, how creamy the stout, how delightfully appropriate the bread and butter, when we have attended a Tragic Play!

Hence, horticulturally, I can welcome winter with

gladness, and can thoroughly enjoy its calm repose. I can, with perfect equanimity, bid farewell to my dahlias and chrysanthemums, and can pleasantly drink to our next merry meeting in the silver cup which they have won. I can bide my time, patiently and thankfully, until the spring-light wakes my cinerarias to bloom, and bids my hyacinths yield their poesy of fragrance. My appetite craves for no stimulants, and asks no artificial food. It desires to say grace, and to rest, that it may be hungry again and healthful, when nature shall prepare the feast.

If ever I grow a-weary—a-weary of my leaflessness and clayitude—good winter hath two ministers, hope and memory, who never fail to cheer. I have but to close my eyes, and memory displays once more before me those banks and braes of beauty which I saw at the Flower Shows, at Kensington, "the Palace," and "the Park;" I am gazing again upon the roses at "the National," the carnations from Slough, the rhododendrons of Waterer, and on gardens in their summer sheen. Or hope speaks musically of the future; points to those dear little cuttings, so bravely upright in their tiny thumb-pots; so charmingly conceited at having roots of their own, and tells of their growth and glory.

And I never realize more pleasantly, or appreciate more gratefully, this welcome rest and happy thoughtfulness of winter, than at the meetings of our little society, which we call "The Six of Spades." Come with me, reader, into our club-room, and let me introduce you to the members.

That club-room is my garden-house, a warm and

cosy chamber, I can tell you, or what would happen to those seed-bags hanging around, or to those roots and tubers piled, dry and dormant, in the background? The adjuncts of the apartment might not, perhaps, impress any but a floral mind with an idea of beauty. There is a potting-bench beneath the closely-shuttered window, with a trowel protruding from such well-matured and mellow soil, that I have heard my gardener declare it to be "as rich as a plum-pudding." Hard by, two bulky bags of sand from Reigate lean lazily against each other, like two aldermen of extra corpulence going home after a Lord Mayor's feast. Beyond is a pyramid of boxes, with many a railway label on their green exteriors, to tell of the anxious miles they have travelled with auriculas, pansies, carnations, verbenas, roses, hollyhocks, and dahlias, in the sunny days that are past. Then comes a solid quadrupedal desk, full of catalogues and secretaries' letters, schedules, and floral publications, good store. Next to it the painter's studio—a table with pots of green and white paint, and neat "tallies," and slim training-sticks, and circular wirework, balloons, and baskets of a dozen fanciful designs. Upon the whitewashed walls a pair of bellows appears to be discoursing with a "Brown's fumigator" on the best method of getting rid of aphides. A wrathful canary, roused from its slumbers, twitters expostulations from its cage, and wishes "The Six of Spades" at Jericho. Above the fireplace is a piece of broken looking-glass, before which I once saw an under-gardener attempting to shave himself with a new budding-knife, and making such grimaces of direful but unconscious ugliness, as would have established the reputation of a clown for life! On either side of this mirror, but deserving a better place, are some of Mr. Andrews's charming delineations of flowers and fruit—among the latter a bunch of grapes, once so lifelike and luscious to look upon, that they might have been the identical bunch which the American artist painted for his mother with such extraordinary power, that the old lady was enabled to manufacture from it three bottles and a half of most delicious wine; but now sadly disfigured by dust and smoke, and rapidly changing their complexion from pale Muscadines to black Hamburgs. Yet more precious the prize cards commemorating the victories won on the tented field.

And now all is in readiness for our conclave, and the members of our small society arrive. Before our blazing fire, which roars a hearty bass to the mirthful tenor of the kettle, is a table for our pipe and glass, behind that table a roomy garden-seat, which will accommodate four of our party, and on either side the fireplace a spacious comfortable chair, the one allotted to myself as president, and the other to Mr. Oldacre.

Mr. Oldacre is the gardener at the Castle, and a "grand old gardener," too, you will admit, as he takes off his overcoat (he has walked two miles through the park this winter's evening), and shows you six feet of humanity, so handsome and so hale that you feel proud of belonging to the genus man generally, and to the species Englishman particularly. Six feet high and straight as a Guardsman, though he has seen the chestnut trees of his great avenue in flower for seventy springs, Mr. Oldacre is a model of manly beauty, from his neat drab gaiters (our ancestors had calves to their legs, and knew it) to the crown of his "frosty pow." Was ever hair so silvery? Was ever neckerchief so snowy white? Was ever face (what a razor must he have!) so bright, so smooth, so roseate? If the French should ever take possession of this country, and compel us to adopt their unpleasant custom of osculating our male friends, I should first endeavour to overcome my repugnance by kissing Mr. Oldacre on both cheeks. There is a perpetual smile and sunshine on them, and in his clear blue eyes, as though he had lived always among things beautiful, and their exceeding loveliness had made his heart glad. What pyramids of pineapples, what tons of grapes and figs and peaches, what acres of flowers, tender and hardy, those hands have tended! The Duke, his master, denies him nothing; and horticultural novelties and floral rarities (things which you and I, my friends, sigh for, and save up for, and speak of with "bated breath," and possess only in our midsummer nights' dreams), these come to the Castle by the boat-load, or travel by the rail on trucks! When you see his soil-yard you imagine that sappers and miners have been at work for weeks, and that an army is about to entrench itself within those multitudinous earthworks. As for his "houses"—houses with enormous tanks, wherein the Royal Lily, Victoria, is waited on by the beautiful Nympheas; houses for orchids, for stove and New Holland plants, for ferns, for fruit, and forcing; his houses of every size and style, from the dingy old lean-to, with its heavy timbers and its tiny discoloured panes, to the grand conservatory, with its spacious dome, transepts, aisles, broad walks, and sparkling fountain;—of these there is no time to tell. Less need, inasmuch as he, whom I now introduce to you, derives not his happiness from his vast material, his unlimited privileges and rare resources, but from his own good and grateful heart, which recognizes God's love and power in all the glorious works around him, and sings

"Non nobis, Domine, sed Nomini tuo,"

for all the sweetnesses and joys of life.

Give the worthy gentleman, for gentleman he is in mind and mien, one of those long clean Broseley pipes. "My dear young Marquis," he remarks, as he fills and lights it, and the pretty little rings of silvery smoke rise upwards from the ample bowl—"my dear young Marquis brought me years ago, from Germany, a meerschaum beautifully carved, in which you might almost boil an egg; and my lord in the Guards, and my lord at Oxford make me presents from time to time of such cigars as I don't suppose are to be bought for money; but my meerschaum goes out when I begin to talk, unless I suck at its amber mouthpiece like a greedy child at a piece of barley-sugar; and the fire of those huge regalias draws so near to my nose, that I grow quite afraid of it; and, in short, I never enjoy tobacco so much as when it comes to my lips, coolly yet quickly, through these long cleanly tubes, and waits for me patiently, as now, through my tedious old man's sentences."

You would like to hear him respond, I am sure, when we drink his health as our "King of Spades," rapping the table with such strong and sudden earnestness as to bring the canary, just hoping to renew his slumbers, very summarily off his perch. "Sixty years ago," he said, in the course of his little speech at our last meeting, "I was weeding the Castle walks. Many and pleasant and prosperous have been my days since then; and if I were constrained to begin life anew I would ask that it might pass as heretofore. But I have no yearnings, though much thankfulness, for the past. There is mildew among our roses here, my friends, and bitter frosts, and dreary sorrowful storms. I hope that I do not deceive myself in thinking" (and here he spoke with such a sweet humility as filled mine eyes with tears) "I trust that I cannot be wrong in believing that, year by year, as I grow older, I draw nearer to a garden of perfect beauty and eternal rest, a garden more glorious than that which Adam lost, the Eden and the Paradise of God."

There was an interval of thoughtful, healthful silence, after Mr. Oldacre had spoken; and we too, my readers, will pause here, if you please, before I introduce to you another member of our club, whom I hope you may like as much as I do—my young friend, Mr. Chiswick, from the Hall.

CHAPTER II.

MR. CHISWICK.

WHEN young Mr. Chiswick, the gardener at the Hall, made his first appearance in our village, he was generally supposed to be an officer of cavalry on leave, or a foreigner of distinction on his travels. Great was the surprise accordingly, when, coming to church the Sunday after his arrival, he took his place with the domestics, and not with the Squire. Nevertheless, though he fell in the social scale, he rose in the estimation of our villagers. Here was a handsome young fellow, with the neatest of moustaches and the trimmest of beards, not come to marry Squire Granville's daughter, and therefore no longer a fascinating impossibility to the more humble maidens around. Mademoiselle, Lady Constance's maid, at the Castle, immediately traced in Mr. Chiswick's lineaments a striking resemblance to the old French *noblesse;* the damsel who assisted at Lady Isabel's toilet was sure that he had been accustomed to the best society; Miss Granville's attendant was forcibly reminded of Lord Byron's "delightful Corsair;" and all our unmarried beauties expressed their true commiseration, "that such a pleasant young man should be buried alive in that lonely cottage belonging to the gardens at the Hall."

There were dissentient voices, of course. Our young men spoke slightingly of "Jews" and "barber's blocks." Mrs. Verjuice, the housekeeper at the Grange, declared his "manners was 'igh, and his appearance 'airy." And even the mild kind-hearted Mr. Oldacre was reported to have murmured something about "a pomological puppy;" to have spoken disparagingly of Mr. Chiswick's "foliage"—to wit, his moustaches and beard; and to have told the Duke's huntsman, that "he would find some excellent covert at the Hall, when he wanted a fox next season." I think that a little breeze of apprehensive jealousy stirred the tranquil waters of that grand old heart. Mr. Chiswick had won medals at the London shows; there was to be a new orchard house at the Hall (poor Mr. Oldacre had only four, well stocked with fruit-bearing trees); and our King of Spades looked sternly (it was but for a moment) from his palace upon the modest vinery of Naboth.

Now what do you think that the King's daughter, at this crisis of our history, the Princess Mary of Oldacre, went and did? Exactly so; for I know that you have guessed it; she did, indeed. As you, my subtle reader, have well inferred, she did *not* wear her second-best bonnet, much less did she distort her very lovely face with unnecessary sniffs and sneers when she met the bearded knight, whom the King, her father, was disinclined to honour. The knight fell head over beard (his ears were planted out by extensive shrubberies, and so I vary the old expression that they may preserve their position of retirement)—head over beard in love with the Princess; and "Jill" (if I may apply such a term to royalty)—"Jill came tumbling after." When Mr. Chiswick got sixty-eight runs from his own bat in our annual match with the Slawmey

Slashers (it is only fair towards our neighbours at Slawmey to remark that their best bowler was unable to attend, in consequence of a very pressing engagement at the treadmill of our county jail), and was carried from the wickets upon the shoulders of his rejoicing and victorious friends, I saw the bright colour rise on Mary's cheek as vivid as the poinsettia; and again, when in our contest with the picked eleven from Moughboro' some clumsy ruffian, shying in widely, hit our pet batsman on the head, and

"Round he spun, and down he fell,"

I saw poor Mary—indeed I went to tell her that there was no serious hurt, having an earnest sympathy with lovers—vainly endeavouring to conceal her sore distress, and as white as a Christmas rose. And so it came to pass, on a moonlit January night, when, in spite of the Under-whip's protestations, that "he never could see the use of them frosses," the Castle lake had been covered with skaters and spectators; it came to pass that Mr. Chiswick, after astonishing every one with his "eagles," and figures, and "outside edge," walked home with Mary Oldacre. And he told her, as they walked, his winter's tale. He spoke of his loneliness in his cottage-home with so much bitter plaint, that you would imagine the Moated Grange of Mariana, or the Haunted House so wondrously described by Hood, to have been quite festive residences, halls of dazzling light, and abodes of the fairies, when compared with his Den of Despair. He described in harrowing terms "the fearful sense of desolation which oppressed him, and would, he knew, oppress him that very evening, when, alone and dolorous in his dreary cave "—(Oh fie, Mr. Chiswick, Mr. Chiswick! how can you thus defame your cosy parlour, with its cheerful fire and singing kettle? How can you thus ignore your horticultural books, your cornet-a-piston, upon which I heard you playing but two nights ago, in your divine despair, the melancholy air of " Old Dan Tucker " ?)—" where no sound was to be heard save the sorrowful sighing of the wind " (he said nothing about the snoring of his small servant asleep in the contiguous kitchen) " and the dismal drip of the rain " (here Miss Oldacre looked up into the cloudless shining heavens, as if wondering wherever the rain was to come from), " he should sit like patience on a monument, smiling at grief "—the monument consisting of a very easy chair, and grief being represented by a plump little pipe of Bristol bird's-eye, and a glass of gin-and-water, " hot with." Finally, this unhappy plaintiff, whom you could not have identified with the smiling skater shooting over the lake only half an hour ago as though he had backed himself to catch an express train, after glancing briefly at the delightful privileges of self-destruction, the repose to be found in yellow fever, and the unspeakable consolation of being killed in battle, in cases of severe disappointment, asked Mary Oldacre to be his wife; and I am quite sure that the bright moon, in all her great experience, never looked upon a happier couple as they came home, hand in hand, and heart in heart, that night, through the silvered grass. Mr. Chiswick returned to his " dreary cave," and evoked unjust suspicions of his sobriety in the small servant, by informing her that "life was ecstasy, and he should raise her wages;" and subsequently proceeded to evoke the sparrows resident in the creeping roses outside with "Love's Young Dream" from the cornet.

You ask, perhaps, at this crisis, with the fast Oxonian in the song, "but what will the Old Governor say?" and I must tell you, in answer, that the primary chilliness to which I alluded soon thawed in the warm bosom of Mr. Oldacre—that he made an acquaintance, and then a friendship, with Mr. Chiswick—and that Romeo knew, when he astonished the sparrows, that he had little to fear from Capulet. And this was so because the younger man ever tendered to his senior that due respect and deference which is not quite so common in these days as it certainly is just and seemly. Mr. Oldacre had expected to meet a supercilious dandy, who would sneer at his superannuated notions, and would expatiate, in a language half Latin and half science, upon the metaphysics of botany, or some pleasant little theme of that sort. He found, on the contrary, a quiet, unassuming, well-informed man, clever, and highly educated in his art, but more anxious to listen than to speak, as one to whom knowledge was teaching her noblest lesson *to be aware how little he knew.* "Mr. Oldacre," he thought, "had not the great advantages which were given to me in those dear old gardens of the Horticultural Society under the wise supervision of 'the Doctor,' and yet how much have I to learn from one who has spent a long life at work, at work upon the best material, and with the most costly tools." And the old man, seeing himself appreciated, was prompt on his part to acknowledge the acquirements of his new neighbour, to exchange information, and to compare old things with new. I met him one morning returning from the Hall gardens, and he informed me that "Chiswick was a regular conjuror." He had just seen him "tie out" a young Pimelea, recently received from the nurseries, and he had made it look worth a guinea! "And the best of it was," he went on to say, "that the fellow had no more pride about him than a dahlia after a hard frost;" and when he praised his handiwork, he only said, "I wish you saw William May's!"*

And thus there arose between these two men, so dissimilar in aspect, yet so congenial in mind, a sincere regard and amity, which deepened into a most true affection, when "the gardener's daughter," quite as lovable as Mr Tennyson's, went over from the Castle to the Hall, and precocious Chiswicks, as time went on, began to drive miniature wheelbarrows between Mr. Oldacre's legs. For the clergyman who made the true lovers one was a true prophet when he said, "Thy wife shall be the fruitful vine upon the walls of thine house;" and whoever enters that pleasant home, once called the Den of Despair, and sees the bright young mother among her laughing little ones, beholds the realization of those other gracious words, preceding the words which I have quoted, "Oh, well is thee, and happy shalt thou be!"

* Gardener to Mrs. Lawrence of Ealing Park, and the best plantsman of his day.

And while the pretty Mrs. Chiswick conducts the nursery department, and every year some "striking novelty" is added to her "hardy annuals," "quite distinct," and a "decided acquisition" in the happy mother's eyes, her husband is making admirable improvements in the spacious gardens of the Hall. His predecessor, old Mr. Woodhead, had been a hard-working man, and a good gardener as far as he went; but he was, metaphorically, a slow horse, more adapted for harness than for hunting, and when he had reached a certain point in horticulture, there he stopped in hopeless immobility, and no spurs could induce him to charge another fence. I remember, year after year, the same plants in the conservatory (ah! those were merry times for the apis, "days of strength and glory" for the red-spider!), the same designs in the flower-garden, the same bouquets in the drawing-room, and the same fruits and flowers upon the table. I think I see his cinerarias now, with their pointed petals (number unknown) widely separated, as though they hated one another. The ladies of the Hall were delighted, indeed, when such flowers as "Lord Stamford" and the "Scottish Chieftain" (I am speaking of favourites in request some twenty-five years ago) displaced these dingy specimens; and yet more gratified were they, when the summer came, and, sitting upon the pretty garden-chairs of Mr. Chiswick's design, they saw the beautiful contrasts of modern taste, Flora's bright jewels set in gold and silver ("Golden Chain" and "Mangle's Silver"), and set so skilfully that, while each separate gem shone in its distinct and glowing beauty, the collective whole charmed the eye with a perfect unity. "Scarlet and goold, scarlet and goold, Tom Thumb and Rugosa Calcy," had been old Mr. Woodhead's motto; and of those he "bedded out" many thousands, making his garden so gorgeous that strange carriage-horses, emerging from the sombre shrubberies through which you approach the house, would actually shy at their sudden splendour; and the vivid brilliancy was so painfully unrelieved and monotonous that it seemed almost to burn one's eyes.

Mr. Chiswick made a hundred other improvements, which I have no time to tell. That damp shaded corner, under the trees of the "Long Walk," where nothing seemed to flourish but obnoxious fungi (they may have been delicious esculents according to the discoveries of modern mycology, but they had not an appetizing aspect), is now, as you know, a fernery; the banks of the lake, which had always looked so drear and reedy, are planted with rhododendrons, which reflect their glories in the admiring waters when the time of flowering comes, and are always beautiful in their glossy sheen; a few trees were felled, and from all the front rooms you can see through the opening our village church in the distance, most striking upon a summer's eve, when its fine old western window blazes and bickers in the setting sun: here is a statue of "Contemplation" admirably posed, with some dark yews, high and dense, for a background, and giving you at once the idea of a place "where ever-musing Melancholy dwells;" there, passing through an arched stone doorway, you find yourself suddenly in Switzerland, where you may spend a day in admiring those charming little alpine plants nestling in the crevices and crannies of the rockwork, and may taste the alpine strawberries if you please, though I warn you that this Arbutus is "Unedo," and that you will not desire to repeat the experiment; and, in brief, you will find, wherever you go, some pleasant proof of a refined taste and an untiring industry.

I must mention just one more instance, perhaps the most decided of his improvements—the transformation which he achieved in "the stove." It was an awful place, that stove, in the reign of King Woodhead; and Mr. Chiswick pretended, when in merry mood, that on his first visit, "a mealy bug, of gigantic stature and ferocious dimensions, had lashed out at him like a horse." Certainly there was more to interest the entomologist than the florist in this remarkable collection. I suppose that the Orchids must have flowered at night, for I never saw them emerge by day from their residences of rotten wood and moss, where they seemed to excrcise unbounded hospitality, and to keep open house for the lower orders of vermin. There were creepers, which declined to creep; sticks trained to enormous globes, but showing no inclination to start upon their travels round them; and plants, on the other hand, which grew like the fairy's bean-stalk—Allamandas, for instance, stretching their arms all over the place, but of flowers "divil a taste;" there were tall thorny Euphorbias about as full of bloom as a hedgehog; there were Begonias with great cracks in their giant "ears," and places which looked as though bitten out by "elephants;" there were Hoyas and Stephanotis, whose every leaf called out, in dying pain, for "Gishurst;" and all the time these helpless, hopeless invalids were insulted and mocked by dirty little "tallies," who persisted with bitter irony in calling them "Bellas," and "Splendidissimas," "Magnificas," "Grandifloras," and "Elegantissimas."

When I see the place now, I cannot recall its former appearance. The Orchids bloom, the Allamandas, the Ixoras, the Dipladenias, the Eucharis, the Stephanotis, the Gloxinias bloom, in all their delicate loveliness; the Hibiscus and Passifloras flower, as they rise in profusion; and the plants of variegated foliage, the Alocasia, the Cissus, the Croton, are models, both in the healthfulness of their growth and in the symmetrical arrangement thereof. Here let us leave Mr. Chiswick, happily admiring a beautiful Caladium argyrites, and pass on to another member of our brotherhood.

Ah, mine old acquaintance, the terror of my childhood, the enemy of my boyhood, the friend and faithful servant of my manhood, are you the next to sit for your portrait? I must have a new piece of canvas, and grind some fresh paints for you.

CHAPTER III.

MR. EVANS.

SITTING next to Mr. Chiswick, whose dark-brown locks contrast with Mr. Oldacre's silvery hair, like Perilla nankinensis with Cineraria maritima, my gardener puffs his pipe. Silent and thoughtful, as one who is wise at whist, he knows every trick in spades, and holds winning cards in his hand. We have scored the honours, have we not, old friend?— in many a floricultural rubber, and proved our capabilities (dare I say our silver cup-abilities?) on many a board of green cloth. Trained in no ducal gardens, taught in no colleges of science, you have learned your lesson, slowly but surely, from the greatest teacher of your art, Experience, bringing to her school that love which she delights to instruct, and which alone can master her laborious tasks. There was never, assuredly, a good gardener yet, who was not first of all a gardener at heart.

My earliest associations with horticulture, recalled as I look upon that old familiar face, were not of a jubilant kind. I have to confess that, at the premature age of five, I gave lamentable proof of my descent from Eve by strong yearnings after forbidden fruit; and that at six I was an experienced felon— no, not a felon, for his crimes meet with capital punishment, and mine were avengéd elsewhere—but, at all events, an artful thief. Neither so expert nor so shrewd, however, as to escape discovery and a just disgrace. My chief strategy, when, a tiny brigand, I prowled the earth for prey, was to enter the kitchen gardens as unconcernedly as possible, and then to call loudly, "Dardner! Dardner!" If he responded I would favour him with one of those spirited comments upon the weather in which we English are so happy, even from childhood, or would make inquiries of a most affectionate (and affected) order as to the condition of his bodily health; and it was, "How do, Dardner? Fine day, Dardner! Dud morning, Dardner dear!" But if there was no respondent in the case, I, the appellant, immediately resolved myself into a Fruit Committee (all articles to be tested by flavour), and proceeded zealously to business.

One dismal day, no reply having been made to my accostals, I had reached the gooseberries, and had taken up my position as a Squatter in (the vicinity of) the Bush, when I suddenly heard with horrible amazement a rustling sound among the scarlet-runners, and like a tiger from the jungle sprang the dreadful Dardner on his prey!

How vividly I recall that awful capture!—the tedious procession to the house, which I did my best to enliven with brisk but ineffectual kicks; the astonished horror of the under-nurse, who immediately foretold my speedy translation to a penal settlement, and could not have expressed herself more severely if I had shot the bishop of the diocese; the trial by Fury, for such the head-nurse seemed to me in her wrath; the solemn sentence, "Put him to bed!" Undressed accordingly (I flatter myself that the operation was attended with some difficulty; there were buttons on the floor, I remember; and the Judge's cap was considerably rumpled), imprisoned, "cribbed, confined," I dreamed a memorable dream. I was in a garden, and a sweet little fairy invited me to climb the magic Bean-stalk. Glorious music from the silver horns of Elfland sounded softly around us as we reached the summit, and as we wandered among the most beautiful flowers and the most delicious fruits. No Dardners marred the prospect; and the fairy pressed me to refresh myself, with an earnestness which I was unwilling to offend. I was regretting, over my fourteenth peach, the lamentable escape of juice, which is so inevitably connected with the outdoor fruition of this fruit, and was meditating a transfer of my attentions in the direction of some white nectarines, when all at once the sunlight faded, and the music was drowned by a thunderous bellowing which shook the "Royal Georges" from their trees. A giant's hand was laid upon my throat; and I awoke to see Nurse at my cribside, standing before me, as Queen Eleanor before Fair Rosamond, with a cup in one hand (rhubarb and magnesia), and a dagger in the other—to wit, a dry old finger-biscuit, which I was graciously privileged "to take after."

You feel for me, reader, don't you? I make no attempt, you will observe, to disparage the seasonable use of physic. I know that Nemesis is the sworn friend of Pomona, and that he who robs the orchard feels justly her avenging gripe. I could forgive Dardner for catching me at the gooseberries, for smiling many a time, as I have no doubt he did, when the doctor's gig drove up the avenue; for the remark he made, on the occasion of my reappearance after a somewhat serious surfeit, that "he was afraid the pretty bird who ate his Morello cherries, had hurt his little beak against the stones;" I could forgive him so far, and I could forgive Nurse for putting me to bed; but to make me swallow that vile nauseous mess, as an antidote to a perfectly impossible stomach-ache, to treat me as one surcharged and plethoric, when I was as hollow, sir, as my own drum; you must agree with me—although the mixture did not— that no insult could have been offered to me with a worse taste, and you will be glad to be told hereafter that I had my revenge. And here, as the champion of injured innocence, I protest solemnly against that flaunting display of the Family Medicine Chest, which I have noticed in some nurseries. The position of our own was fulsome. Each morning it met my awaking sight, with its hard; cold stare of brassy insolence; and it shone in the firelight, when I lay abed at eve, as though polished with the Oil of Castor. The expression of countenance with which the nurses pointed to that box was fiendish; and the way in which they unlocked it, and loitered over the preparation of its doses, was worthy of the Inquisition in its best and happiest days. Somebody filled the keyhole, on one occasion, with an unusual but ingenious combination of coal-dust and batter-pudding; and somebody chuckled in his crib, you may be sure, when Nurse broke both lock and key.

Now let me propose briefly to my brother Spades and others a thought or two concerning the treatment of little children in gardens.

With regard to flowers, let children be taught from the very first to admire, to love, and to cherish them, not to regard them as temptations to mischief, and to connect them only with uneasy recollections of punishment. When Master Johnny decapitates his first tulip, or brings in his first hyacinth, roots and all, from the borders, don't treat him as an abandoned ruffian, and make him frightened at flowers for life; but show him with a calm and gentle tenderness the perfect beauty which his hands have spoiled, and tell him reverently whose work he has undone. Let him draw near and gaze, where he may not gather; point out to him the symmetry, the tints, the perfume; remember that there are organs of Benevolence and Veneration, of Form, Order, and Colour, in the cerebral development of that curly pate, as well as of a Covetous and Destructive tendency; appeal to his higher, holier self, converse with the Christian that is in him; ignore what is evil (for he will understand your tacit abhorrence) until there is stern need of open censure; trust, instead of suspecting; talk to him of prizes, instead of prisons, patting his back with your open hand, instead of shaking your fist at him; and, as surely as Love and Truthfulness are better and stronger than Deceit and Hate, you shall find in that little heart such a sympathy with all things pure and beautiful, as shall bow your head in shame.

With regard to fruit, I should be inclined, I think, to deal with little children as confectioners and grocers are said to deal with their newly-entered apprentices, and to give them a free range. I should, simultaneously, forewarn them thus: "Ladies and gentlemen, you are now at liberty to make yourselves as ill as you please. These sour apples and unripe plums are absolutely at your disposal. You will oblige me by abstaining from the green gooseberries, until I have withdrawn a space, as the *craunch* is painful to my nervous system; but, subsequently, every bush is yours. Your meal will be followed by a variety of aches and pains, for which you will have to swallow some of the nastiest medicines known. These Nurse shall bring to you in a large teacup. If you would prefer to wait until dessert-time, you can have some nice ripe fruit with Papa and Mamma, and a glass of Cowslip-wine instead of Black Dose; but pray please yourselves. Good morning."

They would attend dessert, ultimately at all events, to a man. Bolts and bars tend only to enhance our longings, to excite suspicions in our naughty little breasts that fruits which are so strictly guarded must be of the most delicious order; and each small conspirator whispers to his brother, "It's rubbish, Tommy, about their being unwholesome; they only want them for themselves."

I must tell you now (how one loves to linger even among the naughtinesses of early youth!) how I essayed to avenge myself upon our gardener for his artful ambuscade behind those scarlet-runners. He had, in those days, the finest peaches in our neighbourhood; and upon the occasion of our giving a grand dinner, at which the ducal party from the Castle graciously assisted, he had sent in such a dish of them as could not be surpassed in the county. The specimen which crowned the pyramid was enormous

("Monstreuse," though not "de Doual"), and was the largest I had ever seen, save one, which my eldest sister had made in wax, and in which, so far as size was concerned, she had considerably exceeded the powers of nature. When our guests had arrived (we saw them go through the hall, we little ones, as we stood in our night-gear upon a distant landing, like tipsy Pecksniffs on a reduced scale), and had seated themselves at the banquet, what do you think I had the audacity to do? I stole downstairs, imperfectly accoutred as I was, and substituted the artificial for the real peach, secreting the latter in a cupboard of the housekeeper's room, where the dessert was lying in state!*

Two hours later, some of the ladies were brought up "to see the children." They found me, as you will conjecture, particularly fast asleep. I was located in an inner nursery, which seemed to be regarded that night as a small chamber of horrors, attached to the general exhibition. "Is that the arch-traitor?" I heard Lady Isabel ask; "the villain slumbers soundly! let us kiss the hoary miscreant." And then I heard how successfully my scheme had sped. The pyramid had been placed in the centre of the table, and the big peach had been admired by all. The host had been complimented, as though he did the pruning and the nailing, and general management of the wall-trees himself. The Duke had facetiously suggested that it should be taken to a side-table, and carved like a round of beef. Squire Granville pro-

* This incident occurred long before the introduction of the *diner à la Russe*.

phesied that, when it was touched, there would be such an inundation of juice as would compel the company to swim for their lives. Finally, the Duchess had been persuaded to divide it with her neighbour, and then the imposture was discovered. It had been such fun! Every one had been amused, and the host, though he seemed puzzled and annoyed at first, had laughed most heartily of all.

All this was very successful; but it was not the success I had intended. Not a word of blame was spoken of him for whose entire confusion and discomfiture I had laid my malignant plans. I alone was censured, and that most mildly. Taken by my mother to the Castle, in the carriage and my new clothes, I had expressed my penitence to the Duchess, and had been immediately punished with a large casket of the most delicious bonbons I ever tasted.

Some years afterwards, for the war continued, and "revenge, Timotheus cried," through my boyhood, I made another hostile experiment, which had a completely felicitous issue. Once a-month Mr. Evans, mine enemy, brought in his account-book, and used to sit in an arm-chair by the fire in the servants' hall, awaiting his master's leisure. From an interview of this kind, my father returned one winter's evening to the bosom of his family, in a condition of extreme bewilderment. "Evans had behaved in the most extraordinary manner. Evans, the soberest man on the estate, was ostentatiously intoxicated; could scarcely rise to salute his master, and when he did rise had brought the arm-chair with him, and worn it behind him in the most ridiculous manner. Had never seen any one so demoralized and red in the face. And, to crown all, the man had put himself into a passion, and murmured something about 'standing it no longer,' had sat down with a crash upon his anything but easy chair." There my father had left him; but the first thing in the morning he would have an explanation—yes, that he would.

I could have given him a very full explanation that evening if I had liked. I had smeared the dark seat of that wooden chair most liberally with cobbler's wax, and had limed my bird securely on his twig.

My father sent for me next morning, after a conversation with Mr. Evans on the subject of his *séance fantastique*, and commenced an oration of a severe and admonitory character; but he broke down in his second sentence, laughing till the tears rolled down his cheeks, and leaving me master of the entire position, with the exception of the kitchen-garden, into which I did not feel inclined to wander for many subsequent weeks.

Then came a period wherein we felt that weariness of quarrelling, which the brilliant but bilious Duc de la Rochefoucault has termed "une lassitude de la guerre," in which we still maintained a pugnacious posture, but struck no blows—just as you have seen a couple of pullets drawn up in order of battle, and confronting each other *tête-à-tête*, but wholly indisposed to peck. Alas! I disturbed this peaceful armistice with an onslaught of unprecedented ferocity. An undergradnate at Oxford, I began to fall in love, indiscriminately, with every pretty girl I saw; and Venus must have flowerets for her golden hair, and fragrant posies for her soft small hand. For her sweet sake ("nam fuit ante Helenam," &c.) I commenced such a series of sanguinary raids on the conservatory as must have made poor Evans's heart to "bleed" almost as freely as his plants. Leaders and laterals, hard wood and soft—now the top of a pyramidal azalea, to make the centre of a bouquet, now the first fronds of some delicate and costly fern, to form its graceful fringe—fine old specimens and "nice young stuff," flowers and foliage, all went down in terrible excision, until the place looked as though it were one of her Majesty Queen Flora's jails, filled with plants of an abandoned character, and having their hair dressed à la convict.

Oh, ladies and gentlemen—oh, dames and damsels with your pretty gardens and long scissors of shining steel—oh, gallant lovers, with your trenchant Wharncliffe blades—oh, mothers and daughters, knocking over the flower-pots as you sweep along in your "trailing garments"— oh, wide-sleeved dandies, breaking the young shoots as you reach forth recklessly to seize your prey—oh, belles and beaux, so charming, so amiable, and so profoundly ignorant on the subject of plants!—pause awhile, I beseech you, and stay your ruthless hands, for you know not what fatal mischief you may do. One little snip with those sharp "rose nippers," and you may destroy in a moment the pleasant hopes of a skilful taste, and the just reward of a patient industry. You may ruin the symmetry of a plant for ever; and behold hereafter an unsightly dwarf, when you might have gazed upon a glorious life-guardsman. What should you say, fair lady, were some disagreeable miscreant to intrude upon the privacy of your bright little boudoir, and to extract the tail of your piping bulfinch? And you, my brave gentleman, would your observations be entirely such as your pastor would approve, were you to hear from your groom that some coarse-minded person had paid your stables a visit during the night, and "gone the whole hog" with your hunters' manes?

There is provocation, I must allow, sometimes. There are Spades in the floricultural pack, though not in our company (limited), so mean as to the amount, and so sulky as to the manner, of their donations, that their scared employers dare not, finally, ask for a single petal, and so are led to adopt the facile alternative of freely helping themselves.

But how comes it, the question may arise, that the young Oxonian, of whom we heard just now as at fierce war with gardeners, and as cutting and maiming the plants around him with so much brutal stolidity, how comes it that he has suddenly put off the paraphernalia of battle for the peaceful apron of the florist, and changed his sword into a pruning-knife?

Of this transformation, the happiest event of my life, I must speak hereafter; appropriately, I think, in a little lecture upon roses, which I am preparing at the request of "The Six of Spades;" but I must first introduce you to the rest of our brotherhood; and now, if you please, to that quaint, hearty, honest, hard-working, plain-speaking fellow, Joseph Grundy, head-gardener, coachman, &c., &c., to the good old ladies at the Grange.

CHAPTER IV.

MR. GRUNDY.

I REMEMBER that, when we first formed our floral brotherhood, I introduced the name of Joseph Grundy with some anxiety, lest it should not be welcomed as I wished. I was afraid that his occasional wanderings from the garden in the direction of the stable-yard, the sudden transfer of his attentions from his horse-radish to his horse, and again from his cob to his cobnuts, might disqualify him from becoming a member of our little guild of gardeners. These noses, I reasoned, accustomed as they are to orange-blossoms, will inevitably turn up at the mere notion of a groom with straw at his boots. But those noses did nothing of the kind. My nomination was received with hearty approval. "If he is not too much engaged," said Mr. Oldacre, with a quaint gravity, "in hybridising, or in his 'Botanical History of the World,' let us have him by all means. Seriously, I am glad to second this candidate. While we teach him something about gardening, we cannot fail to profit in turn from the presence among us of an industrious, a happy, and a righteous man."

To these commendatory epithets, I would append the adjective *cheery*, as characteristic of one who is not only happy himself, but communicative of happiness to others. I never meet that Fourteen Stone of healthfulness, crowned with its rosy smiling face, as bright as a good conscience and brown soap can make

THE SIX OF SPADES.

it, without feeling a certain freshness at heart—a braver confidence in the hopes and joys of life—a more sure emancipation from its cares and sorrows. Like the "bit of blue" which precedes the sunshine when the storm-clouds break, that face beams with fine weather. Here is a delightful barometer, which disdains the influence of atmosphere, rain, and wind, and boldly assures you in the middle of a hurricane, that everything is "set fair." It is a face at which babies of the most reserved and haughty disposition immediately smile and coo; while the most timid children "walk under his huge legs and peep about, to find themselves dishonourable" lollipops. Coming quickly round a corner, upon a recent occasion, I suddenly confronted Mr. Grundy, engaged in the arduous evolutions of hopscotch, and his expression of bashful uncertainty whether he should resume his position as a rational biped, or go on with the game and win it, was a supreme treat, I can assure you. Finally, he got upon the line—I wonder with those boots of his that he was ever off it—and resumed his original standing in society, amid the derisive cheers of his small competitors.

You would scarcely imagine that this festive countenance could ever be regarded with a qualified pleasure, nay, even with feelings of discomfort; but there are scenes and seasons wherein I have met it with much perturbation of spirit. I maintain that upon occasions of national humiliation, upon Ash-Wednesday and other days of penitence, Joseph Grundy ought to sit in the vestry. No member of our congregation is more in earnest than he; but his face utterly declines to identify itself with any internal seriousness, and glows in its amazing joy and radiance, as though protesting against the whole proceeding, and contradicting every word of the service.

And was not that same hilarious visage a sore trial and stumbling-block, when, in days that are past and a gallery that is pulled down, Joseph Grundy performed on the bassoon? He was but poor company as a musician, was Joe, but thoroughly conscientious; and though I never knew him to finish with the choir, he always played out his verse honourably, and came in a few notes behind, blown, but extremely gratified. We have an organ now, and the bold bassoonist sings, and sings well, in the choir. Drowsy indeed must that believer be who does not start in his bed upon Christmas morn, when Grundy, lustily and with a good courage, bids his brother "Christians, awake!"

Lustily, and with a good courage, is his rule in all things. It does one good to see him at his work, and I think of the American's striking words of "the nobility of labour, the long pedigree of toil," as I watch him, manfully accepting that irksome destiny, which the first gardener hath entailed upon us all. A right honest Spade is Joseph. His no "lubbard labour," of which Cowper, in "The Garden," speaks as "loitering lazily, if not o'erseen." If you come upon him when he is resting awhile, he does not hastily resume activity, and so confess that he has been idle, and does not deserve relaxation (I always distrust those demonstrative gentlemen who are so excessively energetic when their employer is present), but he stands at ease until he feels himself refreshed,

and then plies his spade once more with a determination
and energy which induce the idea that he has solemnly
pledged himself to dig to the Antipodes before tea-
time. It is good, I say, to watch him at his work,
for "*laborare est orare*," and that work is prayer is as
true a text this day as when it cheered the hearts of
those toilsome monks, who were long the only, and
always the best, gardeners.

So we, having seen Joe Grundy dig, were glad to
admit him into our Society of Spades. He is not
scientific, it is true. I recall mistakes in his nomen-
clature of plants, discreditable to its etymology. I
have heard him speak, for instance, of *yallermandies*,
camelcons, *dolphiniums*, and the like. I know that in
spelling cactus he leads off with the letter K; and I
am quite sure that he could no more repeat some of
the delightful titles which are given to flowers (let me
mention, by way of a nice little specimen, Siphocam-
pylos manettiæflorus) than an Ephraimite could say
Shibboleth. But there is a nobler language, my
friends, than is to be found in botanical dictionaries,—
grand words of Truth, Goodwill, and Honesty; and
these Joseph Grundy speaks. There is a higher task
appointed than the precise orthography of tallies,
that we "learn to labour and to wait;" and he
studies this lesson well.

In his little intervals of leisure, the semibreve rests
of his solo on the spade, during which, to quote his
own expression, he is engaged in "catching his
wind," he is wont to survey with much contentment
the pleasant garden around him. It freshens him, he
says, to have a peep at the flowers, and to see things

looking comfortable and happy, as though they thanked him for his trouble; and, indeed, to look upon that smiling pleasaunce is a "refreshment to the spirit of man." It is laid out much as gardens were a quarter of a century ago. Large beds, round or oval principally, with flowering trees in the centre, the lilac, the acacia, the laburnum, the almond, and their kind; next these the glossy evergreen, the arbutus, the aucuba, the box, the berberis, the juniper, holly, and yew; and outwardly the border for flowers. "And gravel walks there for meditation" meander about these beds in tortuous course, conducting you to sweet little spots of coolness and seclusion, and giving you a continual change of objects for contemplation. I never wander in those charming grounds but I ask myself this question—Are we not making a "tremendous sacrifice" (as the drapers say, when they are anxious to dispose of surplus stock, or seedy old "shopkeepers") to that Gigantic Idol called "Bedding-Out"? Are not our modern gardens, and these close to our windows, fireworks and kaleidoscopes for three months in the year, with brown fallows for the remaining nine? Don't talk to me about your "Winter Gardens," your golden hollies with eight leaves, your priggish little Irish yews, about as big as ninepins. To the nursery, say I, with those tiny infants. And I won't listen to any nonsense about "grand display of bulbs in spring!" The grand display costs a fortune, and comes up "patchy," after all. I looked out the other morning from the window of a grand house in these parts, where they have streets of glass and regiments of gardeners, upon a magnanimous but unhappy experiment to beautify the beds with bulbs. There were to be Maltese crosses in silver, and golden coronets upon cushions of purple. The idea was gorgeous, but the result was this—I could scarcely shave for laughing! Oh, the gaps and the blanks, the *hiatus valde deflendi!* Puritanical mice had defaced the crosses, and appropriated the Crown Jewels.

Surely it is better for mind and body to feed regularly upon wholesome food, upon the meats and fruits of the earth in their season, than to have three months of feasting, and nine of fast. At the Grange there is always something close at hand, not exiled to the kitchen-garden, to please you.

> "The daughters of the year
> One after one through that still garden pass,
> Each garlanded with her peculiar flower."

From the cheerful parlour, with its oaken panels and large square stone-mullioned window, I see in winter the laurestinus, the bright red berries of the holly, the pale-yellow aconite, the white Christmas rose. There are violets under that window, waiting for a sunny gleam, and the room itself is redolent now with the delicate perfume of the chimonanthus fragrans. Soon they will have in abundance the snowdrop (our lady's flower)—the crocus, purple, and gold, and white (the latter irreverently termed by children "poached eggs," and very like them),—hepaticas, the sweet mezereon, and all the first flowers of spring. You " would remove that ribes, because it must look shabby in the winter!" But don't you see that there are too many evergreens around to allow the eye to rest upon it, much less to be offended by it; and that it is so with all the deciduous trees.

"And we seem," said Miss Susan to me (two maiden sisters live at the Grange, Miss Susan and Miss Mary Johnstone, so sweet-tempered and good and graceful, that I often wish they were twenty years younger, and bigamy more in vogue)—"we seem to have all the happiness of a garden, without those little vexations and disappointments which trouble some of our neighbours. We ought to be very thankful;" and I know that she is thankful, though she neither groans, nor squints at the firmament, and in fact does not care what I think on the subject; "for our home is not only lovely in our own eyes, but seems to endear itself to our friends also. Even strangers are struck at once with the greenness and quietness of our 'fair ground.' Our good Duke, lunching here in September —it is only in the partridge season that we have the privilege of a visit—looked around, and sighed to himself, 'How very, very peaceful!' He was comparing our pretty little plot, I fancy, with his grand terraces, and his geometrical designs, his rainbows, his ribbons, and his stars, and I verily believe that he preferred the former. Indeed, he confessed as much, by quoting two lines of poetry, which we afterwards found in a translation by Mr. Pope from Martial:—

> 'But simple Nature's hand with nobler grace
> Diffuses artless beauties o'er the place.'

And dear Mr. Oldacre, the first time he smoked a pipe in the new arbour, seemed to arrive at a similar conclusion. 'Prettier than anything we've got,' he grunted. 'If a man wants to know what a fool he is, let him go and lay out a garden!'

"And it is a comfort to feel that our old-fashioned style evokes neither jealousies nor comparisons from your anxious modern competitors. If the spirit of any young gardener is troubled at the sight of some to him unknown novelty, and envy with malignant glare is eying it, as Greedy Dick the tartlets and pies, he is at once appeased to hear that it has been with us half a century, and is only annoyed with himself for admiring anything so superannuated. No one points out, with lively satisfaction to himself, those 'sad mistakes in arrangement of colours,' which your great artists are as prompt to see in others as they are to overlook in their own parterres. We are never told that our favourite plants are 'quite superseded, and gone out of cultivation some years since!' And nobody sneers at our boiler, for the simple reason that we have no greenhouse. Ah! I must tell you what dear Mary said " (Miss Susan, you must know, looks upon Miss Mary as a combination of Sydney Smith and Venus), "when Joseph expressed a wish, the other day, that we would set up what he called 'a bit of a Consartive-Tory.' 'Joseph,' she said, 'so far as I am concerned, I feel more disposed, as I'm losing my hair, to set up a bit of a *Wig!*'

"And apropos of Grundy, what *do* you think that delightful elephant did last evening? We had a few friends to dine with us, and it unfortunately devolved upon Joseph to place a pyramid of jelly upon the table. Carried unsteadily, it commenced, of course, a series of the liveliest oscillations, and so swayed itself to and fro, when it reached its destination, that poor Joseph called to it in real agony of mind, 'Who-a, who-a, who-a!'* I need not tell you that he concluded the performance by hissing violently, when he swept away the crumbs, as though manipulating his horse—for that, you know, he always does."

And thus those gentle ladies survey with an amused benevolence the anxious difficulties of their faithful Joseph. Who, indeed, could be seriously angry with him, beaming, as he does, from a desire to please, and glowing with a determination to do his best? If on your coat some venial gravies fall, look in his face, and you'll forget them all. He impinges, I confess, upon his fellow-servants, at times when their equilibrium ought to be especially respected—as, for instance, when they are engaged in the administration of coffee, in the setting on of lamps, and the like; but only from an earnest, affectionate wish to hand you your muffin hot, an anxiety to get at you with something to eat—a noble sympathy, which, to feed you, my friend, kicks the shins, treads upon the corns, and ignores the proximity of meaner men. You do not approve, and I do not justify, the deep immersion of his thumb in the Trifle, as he places it proudly before you, although his Berlin glove is of snowy whiteness ("I would I were a glove upon that hand," whispers your comic neighbour, "that I might kiss those sweets"); but we must both of us admire his atten-

* This occurrence in real life was told by me to John Leech, and was admirably represented by his pencil in "Punch's Almanac."

tive care of that beautiful crystal bowl, which he insists on carrying, to the intense terror of the whole household, knowing, as we do, that rather than break it, Joseph Grundy would prefer to be "set quick i' the earth, and bowled to death with turnips."

Only once, within my cognisance, has he been seriously, nay sternly, censured; and this on the occasion of an appeal which he addressed to Miss Susan for the loan of a certain single-barrelled gun, "to shoot them oudacious blackbirds." He affirmed that they not only stole his fruit, but that, when he drove them away, they just "popped on to the top of the wall, and then turned round and *sauced* him." He had invented scarecrows of such repulsive aspect as would have scared, he was sure, any decent birds into fits; but those brutes had come back, " as imperent as imperent." One effigy, that of a gentleman fully armed with the artillery which Joseph desired to realize, and threatening grim destruction to all around, they had treated with conspicuous scorn, sitting upon the fowling-piece, "disgesting," as Mr. Grundy said, and using the entire creation as a kind of lounge, and worse. So had they exceeded in effrontery those, their naughty brothers, of whom we read in a delightful modern biography* that when the ladies set up an old packing-case, with a piece of red bunting affixed thereto, as an object which could not fail to dismay the winged banditti of the neighbourhood, "they stood upon the box to eat the cherries, and then wiped their beaks on the rag!"

* The Life of Patrick Fraser Tytler.

Were not these provocations sufficient, think you, to disturb even the placid spirit of a Grundy, and to make sour within him the rich custards of his human kindness? A mouse, we read, set the lion free; and a blackbird may rouse the British ditto, even as the twopenny tin horn of the bird-tender may excite the startled hunter, or speak to the charger of war. So there he stood, erect in all the majesty of wrath, bold as Ajax defying the lightning, and suggesting that he should like a gun.

And wherefore is Miss Susan mute? Stands she aghast, astonished, speechless, at the indelicate behaviour of the feathered tribe, or wherefore is she dumb? She loved those blackbirds well, and now she wears the strangely piteous look of one hearing, for the first time, harsh things of her beloved, and listening to the most respectable evidence that the joy of her soul is a thief. There she stands, grandly indignant, like the Lady Ida, when she found three men in petticoats among her "sweet girl-graduates":—

> "A tide of fierce
> Invective seemed to wait behind her lips,
> As waits a river, level with the dam,
> Ready to burst, and flood the world with foam."

But Miss Susan keeps the flood-gates closed, and without a word, the heart's stream too flush and deep to ripple, she walks slowly, sternly to the house.

But it is not the birds, my reader, who have caused this sad dismay. It is "animal implume"—it is Joseph Grundy, for whom this stillness in the air portends a thunder-storm. Two hours afterward it fell.

I must tell you, first of all, that a real shower, material, not metaphorical, had just refreshed the earth, and all the leaves of the glossy evergreens were shining, "as if" (Mrs. Verjuice beautifully said) "every one of 'em had been French-polished," when Miss Susan went forth to speak her mind. Poor Joseph's mocking bird was singing on the tree, as though he had wet his whistle to some purpose, and had clarified and strengthened his throat with raindrops, as the operatic songstress with stout.

> "Then Ida, with a voice that like a bell,
> Tolled by an earthquake, in a tumbling tower,
> Rang ruin, answered, full of grief and scorn."

"Grundy," she said (he told me subsequently, with intense pathos, that she had not addressed him by his surname since he upset "them gold fishes" fifteen years ago, and he would much have preferred that she had commenced with "Pickpocket"); "Grundy, be good enough to listen to that flute, and tell me which particular tones are inferior in sweetness to your big bassoon. And tell me at the same time, Mr. Joseph" (he would repeat the "Mr." with an extreme disgust, as though it were an epithet too vile and dreadful for any but the most confirmed garotters), "tell me why that chorister in his black cassock should not sing his anthems all the year round, as you once a-week in the choir. It may be my want of taste, Joseph Grundy, but I prefer the tune which he is now singing to any which I have heard you play. *Shoot the Blackbirds!* Kill our Minnesingers!

I will not dwell upon the perils which must result both to life and property from your first experiments with a gun; I pass over the trifling inconvenience of our compulsory residence in the cellar while you broke every pane in the house; but I pause to ask you how you dare to propose the murder of those sweet musicians, who not only sing for you as you work, but eat your grubs and wireworms by the bushel? Cover your cherries with nets, Joseph Grundy — and your head with shame! You are worse, I declare, than that dull yahoo from the mining districts, who, coming to spend a few days in the country, 'could not sleep o' nights for them nasty nightingales.' Shall I take our cage to Verjuice, and order her to make you a canary dumpling? or would you prefer that four-and-twenty blackbirds be forthwith baked in a pie? Seriously —do those birds no hurt. 'Taught by a Power that pities me, I learn to pity them;' and I commend the lesson to you."

Then her neat figure, in its grey silken dress, moved away upon the gravel homewards; and he was left lamenting. And now befell a visitation, too common in an unloving world: a lancer rode forth to prick the wounded; a donkey came to kick the ailing lion. Like a pirate upon some hopeless wreck, sweeps down Mrs. Verjuice upon Joseph's grief. With bad taste, and worse grammar, she announced her solemn conviction that it was his, Joseph's, desire and haim to break his missusses' 'arts, and it was her opinion, though she judged no one, that he was in Co. (by which she meant in partnership) with most of the internal powers; and she only hoped he might not some day find himself where the worm never should be squenched. This and much additional rubbish she discharged with great volubility, and then, imitating her mistress, retired with dignity.

But distinct and separate, as the orators themselves, were the effects of the two orations. Miss Susan's speech left her hearer sad, ruthfully penitent concerning the blackbirds, and as thoroughly ashamed of the subject, as the Ancient Mariner must have been of the albatross hung about his neck. Mrs. V.'s remarks appeared, on the contrary, the rather to cheer and comfort him; and he so far regained his animal spirits as to wink, when she finished, to an attendant robin (presiding, like an Emperor, over his Diet of Worms, hard by), and pointing with his thumb towards her retreating form, to murmur, "Sing on, Beauty!"

They are good friends, nevertheless, these two fellow-servants; and Sleet and Sunshine, as Miss Mary calls them, enjoy together life's April day. "When the old gal is on the hig," says Grundy—irreverently alluding to those seasons in which the lady's temper is especially acetose, her observations of the pointed order, and her enunciation so exceedingly nimble, that, as Schiller said of Madame de Staël, "a man must be all ear to follow her"—"when the old gal is on the hig, I never counterdix nothink. Beautiful, says I, as if I were admiring of a pin-wheel; and off she goes, just like one, a blazing, and fizzing, and spluttering, till all her gunpowder and brimstone's burnt out, and she stops as still as a hyster." Artful Joseph! shrewd in thy reticence, as the monk Eustace with Elspeth Glendinning, when he remembered that a woman of the good dame's condition was like a top, which, if you let it spin untouched, must at last come to a pause; but, if you interrupt it by flogging, there is no end to its gyrations!

At an earlier period of their acquaintance Joseph had essayed by various demonstrations to intimate to Mrs. V. that her monologues were a little tedious, —yawning with extended arms, and consulting his watch from time to time in a very anxious and ostentatious manner. Such a watch! After an entire derangement of the owner's vest, a liberal display of brace and button, and some powerful tuggings at a steel chain, out it came from its well, like the diving-bell at the Polytechnic. Mr. Chiswick pretended to covet the case, as "a sweet tank for the Victoria lily," and affirmed that when Grundy travelled on the rail his timepiece was charged as extra luggage. But the exhibition of this huge chronometer, displayed and brandished as some intimation that time was on the wing and precious, by no means produced the effect proposed. "The old mare" (you must really excuse Joseph's stable mind) "began to rear and plunge like anythink; and says I to mysen, this here's a hanimal, which she'll stand no ticklings by whips nor straps, and if you don't give her her 'ed, Joe Grundy, you'll be having her heels through your splashboard!"

If evidence were required to show the prudence of these reflections, and I wished to demonstrate the happy consequences of allowing the old mare her head, I should point triumphantly to the scarlet "comforter," which, coming through foul weather to "The Six of Spades," Mr. Grundy is wont to wear, and which was wrought expressly for him by the swift needles of Verjuice. Mr. Oldacre never beholds this neckerchief without addressing an inquiry to the curate (of whom anon, my readers), "whether he is aware that one of the Society has serious thoughts of petitioning Parliament to legalize marriage with grandmothers;" and then he will address the brother in question, and promise him a dish of "the Duke's potatoes," whenever they are needed for the wedding-feast.

But what does he mean by "the Duke's potatoes"? A good many years ago, when Joseph Grundy first came among us, with horticultural experiences of a very limited range, he was invited to attend a general meeting of our Floral and Cottage-gardening Association. The proceedings terminated with a supper, and at this supper were handed round some Jerusalem artichokes, which Mr. Oldacre had kindly sent from the Castle. Now Joseph is a very impartial feeder, accepting all things (I was compelled on one occasion sternly to reprove a facetious waiter, whom I caught winking at his assistant, as he offered to my friend the sweet pudding-sauce, and watched him pouring it liberally all over his boiled rabbit)—and he now helped himself accordingly. Presently an expression of extreme disrelish passed over his rosy face, and beckoning to the landlord of our village inn, the Gunter of our feast, he asked, disdainfully, to be informed, "whose swilltub he had robbed o' them things?" The reply was, that they had come from the Castle, a present from Mr. Oldacre. A momentary surprise and hesitation flitted over Mr. Grundy's lineaments, and then he spoke bravely, as he ever does, his thoughts:—"Duke or no Duke, if poor ould chap gets no better taturs nor these, he'd be foine and pleased with a turnip!"

Hence the allusion of Mr. Oldacre. But Joseph is generally ready for him with some amusing rejoinder, and is never, indeed, to be lightly regarded as an adversary in jest and banter. There came a stranger to one of our meetings, I forget by whom introduced, and who must have possessed, if phrenology be true, so large an organ of self-esteem as considerably to perplex his hatter. This gentleman was pleased during the evening to turn his attention to Joseph Grundy, and, rightly inferring from his appearance that he was not a highly scientific gardener, to inquire, in ridicule, "what orchids he thought of exhibiting at the next Crystal Palace Show?" J. G. took four long pulls at his pipe, and then answered very meekly, "I haven't no orchids, if you please, sir, and I'm not much of a shower; but I think I know what prize you'll win." "Indeed!" said our visitor, evidently pleased with the notion that his fame as a florist was known to us all; "and which may that be?" "Well," said Joseph, "thou'lt be first i' cockscombs, and thou'lt not be very far behind i' greens."

CHAPTER V.

THE CURATE.

Upon the occasion of our Curate's first appearance as a member of "The Six of Spades," I derived much gratification from contemplating the deportment of Joseph Grundy. No sooner did he see his pastor, than he made an uncomfortable attempt to hide his pipe, which, being a Broseley of robust proportions, declined to be concealed at any price; while his features assumed, so far as their mirthful make permitted, a troubled and solemn aspect. Whether he thought it probable that he should be called upon to oblige the company with a hymn, or whether he was under the impression that clergymen were painfully affected by tobacco, after the manner of the green-fly, there was but brief time to speculate ; for the Curate, noting his perplexity, forthwith proceeded to dispel it by filling and igniting an ample bowl of clay, and by taking his seat, next to Joseph, with a pleasant and friendly smile. "I met old Michael Willis yesterday," he said, "and as soon as he saw me, forgetting, I suppose, that he has not a monopoly of eyesight, he swiftly put his pipe in his pocket. So, after some little conversation, I suddenly expressed, to his great surprise, the anxious hope that he was insured. For if," I continued, "the old saying be true, that where there is smoke there is fire, your waistcoat-pocket, Michael Willis, may soon be ready for the tinder-box. And you would be rightly rewarded for doing that which you are ashamed of doing, and for attempting to deceive a true friend."

"I'm not ashamed o' smoking," he answered; "but they do say as parsons hates it."

"Cruelly, despitefully, and with lying lips, Michael. With the exception of a very small company, not conspicuous for liberality or learning, the English clergy have never spoken against the moderate use of tobacco. The majority of them, smokers themselves, would be hypocrites to do so; and of the remainder, they who go much among the very poor, and know how few their comforts, how many their hardships, must be glad to see the enjoyment (not the abuse) of a cheap and innocuous pleasure. They who denounce it must give up all their luxuries, and nearly all their comforts, before they can do so consistently; and then, Michael, we will argue the matter on the principles of religion and common-sense. We have smoked our pipes for three hundred years in England, beginning with a walnut for a bowl and a straw for a tube; and though a king has blown his "Counter-blast against Tobacco," and yellow Puritans have groaned and snarled at it, it still brings pleasant solace, throughout the land and under it—to the miner toiling for the coal, and to him who sits by the coal-fire's blaze; and leaves men as brave and as good, Michael, as when Ralcigh, or whoever first brought the plant among us, was as yet unborn. So I finished my little sermon; and my friend Joseph knows why I have ventured to repeat it here."

"There's another little sermon, sir," said Mr. Oldacre, "upon tobacco and the pipe, which rescues the memory of one Puritan at all events from silly prejudices on the subject. I mean that quaint, touching old ditty which George Wither sang, and which Frank here" (his son-in-law, Chiswick) "will sing for you, if you wish."

Whereupon was rapping of the table, and a preliminary sipping of gin-and-water, and a rearrangement of limbs into the most easy posture for listening; and then Mr. Chiswick, with a voice very pliable and mellow, sang to us the impressive words and appropriate music of the well-known ballad, "This Indian Weed," &c.

And now, my brothers, do I feel glad at heart that I am writing for those who love a garden. I picture to myself some young Mr. Gallio Noodle, sightless and noseless so far as flowers are concerned, yawning over "The Six of Spades," and saying, "Whart a delightful convocation of snorbs! Parson smoking clay pipes with groom, and dram-drinking with the rest of the company, while melodious gent, who has been digging all day, and has come in, I daresay, all over worms, is halloaing Bacchanalian songs." Let him sneer, as he tosses the volume down, and goes off with his cigar to the stables, for I am perfectly unconcerned and happy—happy in my earnest hope that they whose sympathies alone I crave, will recognize in our little assemblies that brotherly goodwill and amity, whereof themselves know from experience the excellent power and sweetness, and whereby the true lovers of a garden are united in a friendship as steadfast as it is pure, and as universal as Divine Beauty itself.

These lovers of the garden know well, that as "one touch of Nature makes the whole world kin," so one truthful instance of a floral taste, one hearty expression of horticultural loyalty, is acknowledged at once and echoed instantly by a thousand kindred souls. They know of signs and passwords more powerful than those of the Free-est Masons, the Oddest Fellows, the most Ancient Druids—a cosmopolitan clanship, accredited throughout the world.

"Rather flowery," I hear it suggested. Well, yes, I think so; and therefore let us put aside the figurative, and illustrate our theme by fact. One hit, straight and home, is worth half an hour of sparring.

Returning, not long ago, from a visit to some distant friends, I arrived at their nearest station four seconds after the departure of the train; and the engine-driver, to whom I bellowed piteously, not being of a floral mind, and coarsely refusing to come back, I was left, with another of the guests, to amuse ourselves for three hours as best we could. What was to be done? It was ten minutes' walk to the town, and to the town we went. Here was a fine old church, recently restored; but it was locked, of course, and both of us were afraid of Bedels. "Was there a billiard-table?" we inquired of the postman. No, but there was a bagatelle-board at the "Cock and Trumpet," an alternative which did not allure us. So to the chief hotel for luncheon, though we had scarcely breakfasted two hours ago; and here we imbibed some fearful sherry, the which, I verily believe, is lurking in my system now. A cigar; and we seemed entirely forlorn and prostrate; when suddenly my thoughts emerged from their gloominess, like railway-carriages from a tunnel into sunshine.

"Are there any nursery-gardens in the neighbourhood?" I inquired of the waiter, just bringing us, with the best intention, a copy of the *Times*, which we had read two days ago.

"Oh yes, sir," he responded, to my great refreshment; "Budd & Packe's, sir; late Twig, sir. Anybody will show you the way, sir."

Away I sped, my companion following reluctantly, for he was no horticulturist; and having referred to "anybody," in the person of an intelligent baker, we soon reached the gardens; and in five minutes I was perfectly at home and happy in the congenial society of Messrs. Budd & Packe. We sauntered through the houses; we peeped into the frames; we wandered among squares of ever-verdant trees, phalanxes of flowering-shrubs, and regiments of the deciduous order. We admired, we denounced, we compared. "Had I seen so and so?" "Did they grow what d'ye call it?" "Did I know thingembob?" I seemed to have been there but ten minutes, when my fellow-traveller, first attracting my attention with a groan, whispered the information that he "was slightly sick of those confounded sticks, and, if he could find a tank or pool, he thought he should go and drown himself." To which I murmured, "Au reservoir"; and we parted. The hopeless Hottentot! "Those confounded sticks" were the cleanest, strongest, straightest lot of briers I ever saw in my life,—tall standards, and breaking beautifully; and he groaned at them! Groaned at them, and when I returned to the station, with two large baskets of plants, pretended painful anxiety as to my mental state, and entreated me to have an interview with Doctor Conolly.

But never, since that day, have I been in want of pleasant occupation—never since have I suffered that most dismal loneliness, the solitude of a strange city, when circumstances have enforced a temporary sojourn in the neighbourhood of a nursery-garden. With principals, or, in their absence, with foremen, I have fifty topics of mutual interest to discuss; in every garden something new to see; from every gardener something new to learn; and so the hours pass swiftly, pleasantly, and I hope wisely, onward.

Wisely, I believe. For, after all, my brothers, it is the wisdom and goodness of gardening which make it such a deep and enduring happiness. It is thankfulness, reverence, and love, which make our gardens dear to us from childhood to old age, for—

" Love is like the ocean, ever fresh and strong,
   Which the world surrounding, keeps it green and young."

Yes, it is because we cannot really love the beautiful flowers without loving Him " Whose breath perfumes them, and Whose pencil paints;" it is because there lies deep in the heart of man a yearning to recover Paradise, and to rest once more upon the Mount of God; it is because when we cherish tenderly, and watch adoringly, the Creator's handiwork, that we are permitted to "walk with Him through the Garden of Creation;" it is because the life of a gardener is, or ought to be, a religious life—

> "Yea, holy is the gardener's life, for unto him is given
> To be a fellow-worker with the sun and showers of heaven,
> Gently to aid the labours of the teeming mother earth,
> And watch and cherish tenderly her children from their birth;"

it is because the wisest of men, such as were Bacon and Newton, were happiest in their gardens, and spake of gardening, from a glad experience, as "the purest of human pleasures;" it is because men, such as was Wordsworth, have bequeathed to us the certain confidence that "Nature never did betray the heart that loved her;"—it is for these reasons, and many another as true and gracious, that the pleasures of gardening are so great and lasting, and that of the earnest faithful gardener it may be justly said—

> "Thy thoughts and feelings shall not die,
> Nor leave thee when old age is nigh
> A melancholy slave;
> But an old age serene and bright,
> And lovely as a Lapland night,
> Shall lead thee to thy grave."

Thoughts like these insured a special welcome for the Reverend Francis Goodhart, our Curate, as he entered our room of assembly. We were glad to have our pastor's sympathy, and to appoint a chaplain to our little band. Moreover, we ever found in him a cheerful companion and an enthusiastic gardener. You may see ample evidence of the latter charac-

teristic in and about his cottage home; in his
delightful garden, which seems to contain everything
in miniature—a diminutive stove, vinery, and greenhouse, a small bed of American plants, a little
rockery, a wee fernery, a tiny fountain, an intricate
geometrical design on the most reduced of scales.
Pretty creepers, twining about his porch, stoop to
welcome you on your arrival, and the jasmine and
the climbing rose look at you lovingly through the
windows as you take your seat within. Passing
through the hall—lobby would be more truthful, perhaps—you see, generally, a large bowl of wild
flowers, gathered and admirably grouped by the
children of the village school. In the study and
drawing-room are choicer bouquets, either culled
from his own Liliputian conservatory or offerings
from some brother Spade, and arranged, as only
ladies can arrange them, by his beautiful sister, Rose
Goodhart, who shares and gladdens the Curate's
home. At early morn, in the sweet summer-tide,
you may see him, with his scythe in his hand, sweep-
ing down the dewy grass, until the church bells call
him to his daily service ("the wust and incurablest
form o' Popery," according to Mrs. Verjuice), and he
goes through the quiet graveyard, carefully honoured
now, and ornamented with flower and shrub, and
through the chancel-door, by which the rose "Felicité
Perpetuelle" climbs heavenward in emblematic
beauty, into the hallowed courts of our dear old
church. These, too, sometimes are reverently decked
by our Curate and his little band of acolytes, and
"the king's daughter is all glorious within" upon her

greater festivals with flower and branch, just as under the Older Testament—but now, in substance and no more in type—the chapiters were covered with pomegranates, "and upon the top of the pillars was lily work." I like to see the children (but don't tell Verjuice) bringing the long ropes, covered round with evergreens, from their schoolroom, to festoon the arches, and encircle the pillars; and yet more do I delight to watch them hurrying home from wood, and bank, and brook, with their pretty posies in their hands. It pleases me most to see the fresh spring flowers at Easter, the bunches of primroses and violets smiling at intervals upon the dark-green yew; but those children tell me, and this of course, that the old church is most beautiful upon their own festival, the which, being held upon St. Luke's Day, brings dahlias in clothes-baskets to our Curate, until the glowing glass in our painted windows begins to pale its ineffectual fire, and our frivolous damsels to complain on Sunday that their best bonnets have not fair play.

Our Curate is not only a lover of flowers himself, but a zealous missionary florist. He was instrumental in establishing our Cottage-Gardening Society, which has reclaimed many a waste place from sterility, many a sot from the beer-house, and brought comfort to many a home. I remember Tom Cooper's garden, for instance, as the favoured residence of every known British weed, and as the favoured residence also of the ugliest and leanest pig in the parish. Mr. Cooper devoted his spare time, at that period, to swearing, thick ale, and skittles, and, lightly esteeming a vegetable diet, quite ignored the science of horticulture. Somehow the Curate got hold of Tom, by finding him some work to do ("just like them Jesseites," Mrs. V. remarked), when he was nearly starving, and as lean as the pig which he had been compelled to sell, and then talked him into his "sober senses." And now no labourer about the place has a cleaner, neater bit of ground than Tom. Dock and groundsel, thistle and twitch, which once grew as closely together as the bristles of his neglected beard, have been displaced for lapstone kidneys and cottager's kale, for gooseberry-trees and currant-trees, for the pæony, the sweet-William, and the rose. It does one good to see Tom, when the daylight lengthens, digging and hoeing, sowing and setting; while Tom, junior, proudly holding a brown-paper packet of seeds, scowls at small Jacky for running between fayther's legs; and mother, with her baby at the cottage door, looks on with a thankful heart. And you would have been pleased, I am sure, if, at our last horticultural exhibition, you had seen, as I saw, the Curate, with his hand on Tom's shoulder, congratulating him on the prizes he had won.

Indeed, I think that there are few institutions more healthful, and few sights more pleasant to the eye and heart, than that of a village flower-show. It induces, first of all, that communion of classes which teaches men, more forcibly than schools or sermons can, to recognize their place and duty; and does this with a cheerful ease and freedom very sparse (please to observe the fashionable adjective "sparse," a new shilling, I assure you, in the coinage of etymology) in the assemblies of Englishmen. Orchids, delicately reared in heat, are gathered under one tent with the hardy wild flowers of the field; the luscious grape from my lord's vinery rests upon the same table with the gooseberry, hirsute and corpulent; and as the question is, not which of these is more beautiful or better than its neighbour, but which is best of its kind, which has been most carefully and wisely cultivated; so when men meet together, lawmakers and brickmakers, coronets and "billycocks," the consideration for each to take home with him is this, not whether he is richer in purse or higher in grade than another, because God has put all men in their places, but whether he is useful and good *in himself*. It concerns every man, and vitally, to reflect, not whether he is a duke or a ditcher, for that is prearranged and fixed, but whether his dukery or his dike are in the best available condition.

If it be said that very few will make this inference, or note my obscure analogy, I may lay stress at all events upon the fact that *there is* the communion of classes, pleasantly established, and that from this kindly genial intercourse new sympathies cannot fail to spring. All are in good spirits and good temper to begin with. The Duke congratulates Mr. Oldacre upon that glorious basket of forced fruits, grapes, peaches, nectarines, apricots, worth a hundred guineas in Covent Garden Market; and Mrs. Cooper is still more delighted with a long-legged dusty geranium, which would soon put an end to the pelargoniums at Slough, by causing them to die with laughter, but which, nevertheless, has achieved to-day the third prize for window-plants.

Then comes a friendly fusion of exhibitors. The owner of the soil has hearty words for that occupier who proves to-day that he is not abusing it, and whose neat garden proclaims to the landlord, every time he passes in his carriage, industry, happiness, and the rent gradually accumulating in the recesses of an old stocking. Again I say it is a goodly sight. The people of a village ought to be as one family, and to-day they seem to be so; and when the band of our Volunteer Riflemen—a good band, too, though the performer on the trombone might be accounted somewhat obese for military evolutions—concludes with "God Save the Queen," we feel every one of us that we have met for good, that there are refreshments in life which can cheer and strengthen for many a toilsome day, and that the surest purest happiness is that of men working with the means which are at hand—so ample and so apt, when charity seeks them —to make those around them happy. To some it is, doubtless, an act of self-denial to give up a day to a village show, but the recompense, even here, is sure. Is it not ever so? I remember to have heard from an elderly colonel of my acquaintance that, when a young man, he was in the habit of going frequently for tea and piquet with an invalid aunt, because he thought it his duty. It was an awful bore at first, he said, but he afterwards found in his kinswoman a most genial companion and excellent friend. "I learned more wisdom from that gentle sufferer," he told me, with an earnest thankfulness, "than could be extracted from a platform-load of Puritans; and, though I give you my honour that I always thought, until the day of her death, that she was in straightened circumstances, she left me ten thousand pounds." "Oh!" exclaims the sceptic, with his unbelieving sneer; and I only wish the colonel could hear him. He would repeat his small observation in a very different key.

But where is the Curate? We left him communing with Cooper *père*—he is now with Cooper *fils*. And there can be no question whatever that Tom junior is at this moment the happiest individual out. He has won the first prize for a posy of wild flowers (we call it a bouquet in our schedule, but I like the sweet old English word far better, and so do the little florists), achieving this victory over thirteen competitors, and surmounting obstacles of a stupendous magnitude; for it is currently reported, not only that Billy Jenkinson's mother had been seen, on her return from weeding, with large contributions of field flowers for her sweet William, but further, that Tim Norris's big brother "got all his, and tied 'em up for him." Against these fearful odds, these grand advantages, Tom Cooper has won the day; he has utterly discomfited the mother of Jenkinson and annihilated the large fraternity of Norris. There he stands, reading the card, which proclaims his conquest, for the ninety-third time, a conqueror far more proud and happy than Wellington himself when Waterloo was fought, and all that he hoped was won.

Whence came, I wonder, Tom's taste for wild flowers, and his cleverness in grouping them so prettily ? Ask him, and he will look up with a smile at the Curate, who is even now suggesting to him how he might have made some little improvements; and if you would know furthermore how and when the lesson is learned, ask the Curate, as I have asked, and you will hear his system.

On Sunday evenings, in the summer-time, some twenty boys from the village school assemble, when the weather is fine, at his Reverence's garden-gate. They have been good lads in church and school, or they would not be there; and as our ecclesiastical Spade comes out, with some books on wild flowers in his hand, little blue-eyed Joe Birley plucks him by the coat, and whispers proudly into an ear very promptly inclined to receive the information, "If you please, sir, I said all that big cholic" (collect for the day intended) "to Miss Rose, and never made no mistake." Whereupon Joseph is permitted to carry one of the volumes for reference, a dignity esteemed in that boy brigade as highly as the Victoria Cross by a soldier; and off they go for the fields. At the first stile, which leads to the inclosures, there is a halt for choosing sides, the Curate nominating two of the most experienced artists as leaders, and these electing their forces alternately. Then the subordinates receive from their commanding officer their special orders and instructions: some are to remain with him to help in arranging; these are to gather white flowers, those pink, and so on; while others must bring "totter-grass," fern, or variegated leaf, to complete the outer circle of the collection.

Each company has a librarian, whose office it is to

find in his illustrated works the flowers brought in by his brothers, and to communicate their name and history. Their English names, mind you, for our Curate wisely declines to muddle their small brains, and weary their young jaws, with botany. I never saw him angry but once, and then with a bilious old gentleman, who proposed that all wild flowers exhibited at our show should have their Latin names and classification. "I'll tell you *my* mind," quoth the Curate; "botany is a grand science for those who have the head and the time for it, but it's about as useful to a ploughman's child as a ball-room fan to an Arctic voyager; and therefore, so far from rewarding any of my young rustics for Latinising our dear old country flowers, I should be inclined to award for the precocious pedant transportation to Botany Bay. Carry out your idea and we shall have the labourer's child no more exclaiming, 'Oh, faythur, there's a dandelion!' but 'Aspice, O paterfamilias dilecte, ubi Leontodon taraxacum flavescit!' while his sister, pointing to a buttercup, shall astonish its mammy by requesting her to 'employ her optical apparatus in the direction digitally indicated, and to admire the Ranunculus bulbosus, of the class polyandria, and the order polygynia.'"

"I try to teach them something better about buttercups," he said to me, as I met him one evening with his boys, and he referred to the subject; and plucking one of the flowers in question, he held it before a charming little fellow, who could scarcely have seen half-a-dozen summers, and asked him if he had learned any verses about it. The answer came promptly, in that soft reverential tone which makes a child's recitation so very touching :—

"It would be wrong on pomp or dress
  To spend our thoughts or hours;
Another lesson Christ has taught,
  Showing the simple flowers.

There's not a yellow buttercup,
  Returning with the spring,
But it can boast a golden crown
  As bright as any king."

"That will do," said the Curate. "Now, Johnny," and he called another of his pupils, "tell this gentleman about 'all things bright and beautiful.'" And Johnny began forthwith :—

"All things bright and beautiful,
  All creatures great and small,
All things wise and wonderful,
  The Lord God made them all.

Each little flower that opens,
  Each little bird that sings,
He made their glowing colours,
  He made their tiny wings.

The rich man in his castle,
  The poor man at his gate,
He made them, high or lowly,
  And ordered their estate." *

And Johnny was commanded to cease firing. "They love these verses," our pastor continued, "as they

* These and the preceding verses are from "Hymns for Little Children."

love the flowers; and my hope is, that through life they may connect the one with the other.

"There is a wondrous revelation in these earth-stars, blue and golden, as Longfellow has told us in his grand melodious rhymes, and I trust we are reading it together. I love to imagine that when these boys are men, the labourer going to his work and from it may be reminded, as he looks upon these old familiar friends, of the lessons we are learning now; that "the hewers of wood" may stop to recognize, with pleasant memories of the past and brighter hopes of the future, the anemone, the primrose, the violet, the lily, or the hyacinth; that pale mechanics, in their Sunday walk, may repeat to their little ones the precepts which are taught by the flowers; and that soldiers and sailors far away may dream of the meadow and the grove, and awake with a deeper affection for their beautiful English birthland, a braver heart to maintain its freedom. Yes, I love to imagine that the recollection of these happy wanderings among the summer flowers may help to revive in weary men the freshness of boyhood's happiness; that some of these lads may hereafter be of that company of whom our greatest sacred poet has said :—

> "There are, in this loud stunning tide
>   Of human care and crime,
> With whom the melodies abide
>   Of th' everlasting chime;
> Who carry music in their heart,
> Through dusky lane and wrangling mart,
> Plying their daily task with busier feet,
> Because their secret souls a holy strain repeat; "

and may know, to quote the words of our greatest divine since the Reformation,* how to 'reconcile Martha's employment with Mary's devotion; in the midst of the works of his trade to retire from time to time within the chapel of his heart; and to converse with God by frequent addresses and returns.'

"I want these little men to be what Mr. Kingsley calls 'minute philosophers;' to find by the roadside and by the brookside some of 'the riches which God has given the poor;' to feel, as it is wisely said by Alphonse Karr, in his delightful 'Tour round my Garden,' 'Le bonheur n'est pas une [rose bleue, le bonheur est l'herbe des pelouses, le liseron des champs, le rosier des haies, un mot, un chant, n'importe quoi.'"

And much more pleasant converse had I with our Curate on that sweet summer's eve, what time the happy boys were racing to and fro with the pretty posies in their hands; and the gorgeous kingfisher shot down the brooklet, like a meteor, at the sound of their merry voices; and the swift trout darted to his hole, as they plucked the campions from the bank; and the landrail craked in the mowing grass, complaining, I infer from his harsh tones, that, being long-toed and formed for the swamps, as our natural histories instruct us, he should be thus uncomfortably located in the meadows; and far in the distance "the cuckoo told his name to all the hills," some of them distinctly repeating it, as though Mr. Cuckoo were going upstairs to a party; and we wandered and wondered, until the dews wept for that gentle day;

* Bishop Jeremy Taylor.

and the two floral armies fought the battle of the bouquets, and victory was adjudged; and victors and vanquished supped, "as only boyhood can," upon the Curate's bread and cheese and beer; and we all went thankfully home, and "bedward ruminating."

CHAPTER VI.

THE CLUB IN SESSION.

WITH that anxiety which we ever feel that they whom we like should like each the other, I have essayed to describe carefully and faithfully the members of our little congress; and though I am well aware how easy it is to sketch from nature without being natural, I hope that I have conveyed to genial minds, by which I mean minds horticultural, some accurate presentments, as well as some favourable impressions, with regard to my floral friends. Writing with truth and earnestly, I permit myself to enjoy the pleasant confidence that I may have imparted to my readers some of the brotherly regard and affection which occupies my own heart for the hoar head of good Mr. Oldacre; for the bright, intelligent face of the bearded Chiswick (you should see him in the uniform of our volunteers, as straight and as handsome as a pillar rose); for the shrewd, thoughtful countenance of Mr. Evans, musing upon soils, and "stopping," and training, with a view to future exhibitions; for the shining jolliness of Grundy; and for the kindly goodness of our worthy Curate. And, having this trust as my encouragement, I go on joyously to chronicle our proceedings, and follow up my introduction with a cordial invite that you, my reader, will join us, in imagination and sympathy, as we sit in synod, and will listen leniently to our discursive colloquies.

Be with us, therefore, in those "long nights of winter, when the cold north winds blow;" chair thyself comfortably by our hebdomadal board within the pleasant influence of our glowing fire; charge thy calumet with the soothing weed, and thy crystal with golden wine from "the bright and laughing barley;" while throned on the tiny clouds above us, that sweet little fairy, Queen Fancy, smiles upon our cheerful convocation; and as she waves her magic wand—

"Again the garden glows,
And fills the liberal air;"

again our beds and borders (hard-frozen in reality without and hidden by the snow) brighten in their summer sheen; again every greenhouse stage bears its precious freight of loveliness; again we see our exhibition vans drawn up at the garden-gate, and borne delicately, as though we carried some sleeping beauty whom we feared to wake, the specimen plants so long, so fondly tended, come forth to witch the world; again we await in anxious suspense, during two hours, which seem a fortnight, the departure of the censors, and the opening of the doors; again we draw nigh to our favourites, pretending indifference, and trying to saunter, but painfully eager in our fluttering hearts to know what award has been made to us; again those hearts rise, light and bright as a soap-bubble in the sunshine, as we read the welcome words " first prize," or sink, heavy as an under-boiled barm-dumpling, to find that we are not placed; again we hear, victorious, that happy " All right, sir," from our gardener, and, like a schoolboy just informed of a hamper, can scarce forbear to cheer; again, defeated, we entertain for a moment an absurd conviction that the judges are either in league against us or in a state of hopeless intoxication, soon recovering our better mind, and finally feeling all the more likely to bear fruit hereafter, like beaten walnut-trees, or any other tree, in fact, since each—

> " Sucks kindlier nature from a soil enriched
> By its own fallen leaves; and man is made
> In heart and spirit from deciduous hopes,
> And things that seem to perish."

Such are our reflections and remembrances, and very soon after a few preliminary remarks upon the weather, the news of the great world in general and our little world in particular, we come—

> "Like doves about a dovecot, wheeling round
> Our central wish, until we settle there,"—

to open our hearts concerning them. And it is amusing to note the change that has come over us, now that our tourney is over, and the heavy harness of warfare doffed for the trunk-hose of peace. Can we be the same knights who, whilom reserved and cold and dignified, moved through the serried lists? Can I be that captious florist, who, when dear Mr. Oldacre gave me his "candid opinion," which I pressingly solicited, about my bedding-out (only I did not really want him to be candid, except in the sweetmeat sense), and told me, with other adverse criticisms, that one of my mixtures, of pink and purple, geranium and verbena, was like a leaf from an old blotting-book— can I be the man in whose disappointed breast a malignant voice was permitted to whisper something about a "superannuated jackass"? Alas! I know myself to be so; and I make feeble amends by a tardy thanksgiving to my mentor, and by an acknowledgment to myself that I deserve flagellation from a robust lateral of Araucaria imbricata. And here is Mr. Evans, in a like spirit of meek magnanimity, acknowledging that his dahlias were not large enough, whereas when the judges gave them second honours, he designated those functionaries as "three old scarecrows," and expressed a strong belief that they were only competent to grow groundsel for sick canaries. Even Mr. Chiswick is acknowledging a failure with regard to some choice auriculas, and making to his neighbour the Curate a sort of auricular confession; while wise Mr. Oldacre laughs at us all, well knowing that, when spring and summer come, we shall be just as sensitive, jealous, and contentious as before. "But it's all right," he says, "for you're as honest and earnest in peace as in war; and whether the hand is open for amity or closed for sparring, the heart goes with it. May the best man win!"

Ordinarily, we have no stated subjects for discussion, and we pass from one topic to another as the occasion prompts. We touch promiscuously upon boilers, flues, and stoves; heating, shading, and ventilating; washing, sulphurating, and fumigating; disbudding, stopping, and pruning; tying, training, and packing; manures, solid and fluid; soils, sands, and peat; tallies, ligneous, metallic, vitreous; traps for earwigs, birds, and mice; tiffany, nets, and bunting; knives, saws, and scissors (nothing said about tweezers);—these, with five hundred other matters—for our conversation takes an unlimited range, from a caterpillar to the Crystal Palace—pass rapidly before us, as we sit in conclave, "dreaming the happy hours away."

But for six nights in the year, at Christmastide, we have special subjects for the evening's consideration. Each member of "The Six of Spades" is called upon either to deliver a lecture, tell a story, or sing a song, in his turn. Here is our last programme, and a faithful chronicle of its realization shall be given hereafter:—

"THE SIX OF SPADES.'—Special Meetings.

Date.	Member.	Subject.
1st Evening	The President	Rosa Bonheur.
2nd Evening	Mr. Oldacre	The Lady Alice.
3rd Evening	Mr. Chiswick	On Bedding-Out.
4th Evening	Mr. Evans	Shows and Showing.
5th Evening	Mr. Grundy	Mr. Grundy's Song.
6th Evening	The Curate	The Happiness of a Garden.

CHAPTER VII.

THE PRESIDENT'S LECTURE—"ROSA BONHEUR."

My dear Brother Spades,—Like a herring-boat astern of the Great Eastern, I follow in the wake of grand examples, and commence my essay, as some great essayists are wont to do, with a topic very remotely connected with the chief theme of my history.* For I have nothing to say concerning that wonderful Frenchwoman who has painted, to our great surprise and delight, "The Horse Fair" and "The Denizens of the Highlands," and have only borrowed her sweet name to serve as my text and motto—Rosa Bonheur, *Rose est Bonheur*, the Rose is Happiness, Félicité Perpetuelle, a thing of beauty and a joy for ever.

I go back in happy retrospect to the sunny days of childhood. I wander once more in bowery lanes, what time there were hedges in the land, and ere the face of nature was so closely shaved by the keen razor of improvement. It is the time of roses—wild roses, blooming fresh and fair, from cold soil and thorny stem, like wisdom and hope from sorrow;

---

* I remember the elder Grossmith giving a most amusing account of a lecture which he wrote to test the sagacity of his audience. It was entitled "The Dark Races," but beyond the repetition of these three words at intervals there was no other reference to the subject. The oration was delivered with solemn gravity, heard with deep interest, and vociferously applauded. It began, I remember, "The Dark Races, my friends, the Dark Races! A wheelbarrow is not beautiful, but it is useful."

wild roses, lighting up the land with their pure starlike glory, and beautifying the gloom of a fallen world; wild roses, on which Adam looks, as he toils with the sweat on his brow, and yearns at heart for Eden. It is the time of roses; we pluck them as we pass, and make a coronal, nurse and I, for my little sister's hair. I see her now, enthroned upon some southward bank, where the oxlip and the violet have watched in their season the slumbers of the fairy queen, smiling through her tears, herself a dewy rosebud; for the brier has pierced her small tender hand, and her spirit has been startled, and has quailed awhile, at the presence and the prescience of pain. Only a moment, for the breeze which gently stirs those golden tendrils, and bears away a crown jewel in that petal which flutters to the ground, is fraught with sweet scents and sounds, with frankincense rising heavenward, and psalms from a thankful choir; and all things young and innocent must needs rejoice. Dear days of sacred gladness, fair hours of guileless love! I never see the wild rose now, but I hear sweet whispers of their " tender grace," and I am wandering once more through the bowery lanes, with my little sister's hand in mine.

And next I remember those roses of the garden, which, few and precious, were the delight of my early boyhood; the glorious Provence (that elegant individual who first called this blushing beauty " Old Cabbage," ought to have been imprisoned for treason against the Queen of Flowers, and his diet restricted scrupulously to the humble esculent in question),—

the grand Provence, which came to us, as our roses now, from the sunnier clime of France, the herald of a great and splendid army, the evening star, which glitters for a while alone ere all the firmament is thick set with gems. Ah, my brothers, what a sublime astonishment and ecstasy must this rose have caused when it first arrived in our land! No ambassador, however copper-coloured, no hippopotamus, however far advanced in gestation, could educe such a sensation now. How the French florists must have shouted in exultation, "*magnifique!*" and "*très superbe!*" How the writers and singers of romance must have rejoiced in this fair reality! How gaily, with this flower in his cap, must the troubadour have touched his guitar! The brave knight wore it in his helm, the gift of his ladye-love, and while his adversary was gazing with rapt admiration on it, saw his noble opportunity, and stuck a lance into his ribs.* Ah me! what tender tones, what plaintive heart-music, what hopes and fears have been sighed over this rose of Provence! Beauty hath made for it a second sunshine with her smiles, and Memory has shed upon its leaves her gentle rain of tears. How often hath this sweet messenger been made to tell unto loving hearts a language which they dared not speak! How often by lily hands have its petals been plucked and

* Who has not enjoyed the mock tournament in the ring of the circus wherein one of the knights mounted on hobby-horses suddenly exclaims, "Bal-loon, Bal-loon," and as his adversary gazes upwards perforates him with his spear and prostrates him in the sawdust?

scattered in the wild hours of mistrust or jealousy as Guinevere suspecting Lancelot,—

> "Brake from the vast oriel-embowering vine
> Leaf after leaf, and tore, and cast them off."

Let us ever, my friends, love the Provence rose, not only for its own loveliness and sweetness, not only as the rose *par excellence* of our boyhood, but as having been for more than two centuries the chief grace and glory of our English gardens, the fair favourite (as the rose will ever be, I trust) in every grade and shire; what time upon holy altars, in the halls of kings, in the grand gardens of the nobility, among the few flowers of the farmstead and cottage, it found a place and throne.

Growing near "the Provence" in our garden I remember next a rose, which came to this country together with it, or shortly afterwards, from Holland; —I mean the beautiful Moss; most beautiful, when, like some sweet infant smiling out of its pretty head-gear of lace, or some young girl blushing to show herself before an admiring world, it first displays its loveliness " i' th' bud."

Next in favour to the Provence and the moss, the sweet little "Fairy" rose (Rosa Lawrenceana) gladdened my childhood with its tiny loveliness; and I can see our wax doll, through the powerful telescope of memory, asleep in her miniature crib, with those wee flowerets on her coverlet and pillow. For she was a Royal Princess, you must know, of amazing beauty and of boundless wealth, and rested always on a bed of roses, until she died one day a melancholy death, slowly roasted before the nursery fire by our brother Fred, to spite us. Very pretty are these Pompone roses ; and as at the great poultry-shows there are special classes for the pert, charming, and consequential family of Bantams, so should I like to see at *our* exhibitions a Liliputian box of these mignons, decreasing in circumference from Ernestine de Barente to the Banksiæ.

And the York and Lancaster, flaunting in its colours, but flimsy in its subtance, like some other gaudy " swells " ! It was a delight, I remember, to arrange its petals, few as beautiful, upon a bit of newspaper, place over them some broken glass—(once in a desperate dearth of crystal I attacked an attic window with my battledore, and never since, I give you my honour, do I seem to have done anything half so daring)—and to call the consummation a " flower-show." I thought of those rose-leaves and of the broken pane, when it was my privilege to superintend the third national rose-show in the Crystal Palace ; and I murmured to myself very thankfully, very happily, and, I am afraid, very proudly, " The child is father to the man." Poor old York and Lancaster ! it has almost succumbed to New Village Maids and Œillets Parfaits, and to Perles des Panachées and Tricolors of all denominations, and nothing remains to remind us of it now but the Lancashire and Yorkshire Railway.

I can but recall, in addition to the varieties I have mentioned, a white rose, whose name I never knew, but which bloomed in beautiful abundance, and much resembled Princesse de Lamballe ; the sweet-brier, whose fragrance we were wont to express, with some precocious insight into the perfumery business, by crushing its leaves with our small fingers; and the Old Monthly, which looked in at our schoolroom window, and tapped thereon with its buds at times, as though inviting us, like the lover of "Maud," to come into the garden, and be glad. How we used to envy those happy flowers, rejoicing in the sunlight, dancing in the summer breeze, unconscious of pothooks and hangers, emancipated from the thraldom of high-backed chairs, perfectly indifferent as to the orthography of the word *cat*, and not caring one dewdrop when who was king of where, or which was capital of what! The bees and the butterflies, when they came to call upon the rose, used to laugh, I am confident, at our bare little legs, dangling from the uncomfortable *sedilia* just now alluded to; the saucy sparrows twittered at our state; and the blackbirds, eying us from a contiguous laurel, whistled comic songs at our expense.

They are gone, the roses of my childhood, deposed by fairer flowers. Where those six held dominion absolute, six hundred distinct varieties have unveiled their beauty to the summer moons. They are gone from our gaze, but from our loving memory they shall never fade. I have a group of them, exquisitely painted by the skilled touch of a vanished hand, in a dear old family scrap-book, which I would not give for anything in the Bodleian Library; and I often turn to them with a tender sorrow, a grief which is almost gladness, having a hope as pure and beautiful as they.

And now must I confess, with a blush upon my cheek as deeply crimson as Senateur Vaisse, well described in the rose catalogues as "intensely glowing scarlet," that for some fifteen years of my existence I walked "this goodly frame, the earth," with about as lively an appreciation of the beauties of a garden as may be supposed to be experienced by a collared eel. Abruptly and completely, like a coquette deserting a baronet for a peer, I transferred my affections from Flora to Pomona, and became miserably oblivious of all flowers pleasant to the eye, in my absorbing greediness of all fruits, which I erroneously supposed to be good for food.

I have not, my dear brother Spades, I assure you, one unkindly thought against apples; I have not a detrimental remark to make against gooseberries, however green. Childhood, I know, will distend its little self, boyhood will fill its large pockets, and youth must have its fling (at the pear-tree), whatever age may preach. For myself, so far from sermonising, I thoroughly admire that magnificent digestion which is no longer mine; I fondly desiderate that glorious palate for which no magnum bonum was too unripe; and I mournfully envy those noble grinders which drew the cobnut from his shell, and were not afraid to grapple even with the apricot's iron stone.

But while I speak approvingly of this early fondness for fruit, and say of it, as Sam Weller said of kissing the pretty housemaid, that "it's natur, ain't it?" I see no reason why a fondness of flowers should not be developed contemporaneously, or why in childhood and boyhood, and in many cases throughout manhood too, the sense of sight and of smell should minister only, so far as gardening is concerned, to the gratification of our tongues and throats, and cease to co-operate with the heart and brain. Why should not that love of the beautiful which is innate in every exile from Eden, be encouraged by our pastors and masters, with as much care and attention as the Greek grammar? Why should not our schools—and there are many, thank Heaven, in which refinement of taste is no longer derided, and where it is no longer considered effeminate to avow an admiration of the works of God—why should not these schools have their garden as well as their playground? and why should not those who will hereafter have gardens of their own be instructed in that happiest and most useful of all sciences, horticulture? What arts could be better worth learning than those of making our homes beautiful, of providing ourselves with a never-failing source of innocent gratification, and of supplying to those around us the continual refreshment of delicious fruits, with a healthful abundance of those vegetables which are adjuncts, as excellent as they are economical, to every man's daily food?

From these plaints you will infer, my friends, that I had small encouragement in my earlier years to foster my first love of flowers, and that I received no instruction whatever in the gentle craft of the spade. Once or twice during my schoolhood the old light emitted a feeble ray, and I was so far illumined on a special occasion as to lay out ninepence on a fuchsia. It was received, I recollect, on its arrival from the nursery, with a great profession of regard and admiration from several of the bigger boys, and they proceeded at once to demonstrate their affection by administering a variety of liquid manures, such as blacking, sour beer, and mustard, which they assured me, on the authority of gardeners at home, who had made the fuchsia their special study, would cause an immediate and gigantic growth. But when they proceeded, "according" (so they said) "to the invariable practice at Kew Gardens, and to the principles laid down by Dr. Lindley," to distribute a fire-shovel of hot cinders around my poor little plant, credulity gave place to bitter tears ; and though I had the subsequent satisfaction of definitely discomfiting in five rounds a young gentleman, who thought to improve the occasion by addressing me as a "sniffling softy," I took heart no more, during my scholastic term, to exhibit single specimens in pots.

In the groves of Academus (to use that beautiful diction, which is a trifle more appropriate to the groves of Blarney) there prevailed, floriculturally speaking, as remarkable a dearth as dreariness. Beneath the trees of those renowned plantations, which dip their metaphorical branches in the limpid waters of Isis and of Cam, we grew nothing but scarlet-runners (undergraduates in hunting costume, swiftly darting from quadrangle and cloister to avoid collegiate and proctorial authorities) ; a few stocks (the freshmen wore them, when there was not the same connection as now between a Buckle and Civilization); and a large assortment of bachelors' buttons (straps being the fashion in those days, and wrist-studs unrevealed).

We attended, it is true, with a prompt punctuality the flower-shows in "Worcester" gardens, and no one could gaze more earnestly than we did upon those very delicate roses and tulips which require the protection of a bonnet. We came away, moreover, with quite a longing for heart's-ease, and were ourselves most perfect examples of sensitive plants and of love-lies-bleeding. But all this in figure, and that figure a cipher. We never looked at the flowers, nor thought of them; and when I was asked by a floral friend whether I had seen that lovely polly-anthus, I urged him, to his grand amusement, to point out at once the beauteous Mary, and, if possible, to introduce me. I never met him afterwards but he had something facetious, as he supposed, to say in reference to my mistake: "Should I like to know the fair Hannah-Gallis, the charming Carry-Opsis, the fair Sal-piglossis, the celebrated Miss-Embryanthemum, the two great heiresses Miss Mary-Gold and Miss Annie-Money? Had I seen anything latterly of John-Quil, Bill-Bergia, or Stephen-Otis; of our Scotch friend, Mac-Ranthus, or our Irish friend, Phil-O'Dendron?"

And so, *sans* ears, *sans* eyes, *sans* nose, I wandered flowerless through a flowery world. Some, perhaps, may tell me that it was better so; that boyhood should find its recreations in active games, and youth in the sports of the field; and that floriculture is incompatible with that hardy physical training which hereafter is to make the man. But I designate this doctrine humbug. Why should a boy be less brave or strong if taught to appreciate the beautiful things about his daily path? or why should youth ride more timidly to hounds because it had a flower in its coat? There is a time for all things; a time to tend some graceful plant, as well to kick a football; a time to store the heart with gentle attachments and refined tastes, as well as to run and row; a time to develop the intellectual as well as the physical powers.

At length, to revert to my own history, a brighter morn dawned upon my darkness. A single star, twinkling in the firmament, first told the advent of a jocund day; and that star, my friends, was—A ROSE.

As a look, a gesture, a picture, a song, a perfume, may suddenly transport the mind to things and thoughts forgotten half a life, so did this rose, a Salvator Rosa to me, at once revived that early fondness for flowers which had slept as paralyzed as Merlin in the oak, since my childhood laughed among the cowslips. The ice broke with an instantaneous crash, and set the river free; the fog disappeared before that single sunbeam as swiftly as the spectre army which beleaguered the walls of Prague; and it was summer-tide once more. Anatomists tell us of cases in which the brain, accidentally injured, or otherwise oppressed, has been relieved after long incapacity, and its powers restored; we have an account, for example, in the *Edinburgh Review*, and in an article upon "Brain Difficulties," of a young gentleman whose sagacity was considerably enhanced by a well-timed kick from a horse; and so was I, on an analogous principle, successfully trepanned by Dr. Rose, and my floral apprehension again put in working order. The clock struck only one, but, like the remorseful villain in the tragedy, I remember to have heard a clock strike in my infancy —I am overcome—I burst into tears—and become a virtuous and exemplary character for ever afterwards.

Sauntering in the garden one summer's evening with cigar and book, and looking up from the latter, during one of those vacant moods in which the mind, like the jolly young waterman, is absorbed in "thinking about nothing at all," my eyes rested on a rose. It glowed in the splendour of the setting sun with such an intense and burning crimson, the tints of vivid scarlet gleaming amid the purpler petals, as light in jewels or in dark red wine, that I shall never lose my first admiration for Rose d'Aguesseau (Gallica), although, having accomplished the mission intrusted to her by Flora for my restoration, she has never since appeared in my rosarium in such resistless beauty. But I ever think fondly of my first fair love, remembering among a thousand charmers the darling of my early youth, as the heart of man is prone. Bluebeard himself, I do not doubt, was wont sometimes to muse with special satisfaction upon the fascination of that young lady on whom he first lavished his affections, and subsequently tried his carving-knife.

The next evening found me in my accustomed seat, but my cigar was exchanged for a pencil, with which I was making careful notes, and my book was "Rivers on the Rose." This dear little red book, *couleur de rose*, so earnestly, so gracefully written, in a language which, as Lord Macaulay says of Livy's, is "always fresh, always sweet, always pure" (he might have been describing a rose)—this guide to amateurs, which has brought so much happiness to the neophyte, so much instruction to the learner, so many glad memories and genial sympathies to all rose-growers, quite completed my conversion. In that pleasant manual there is a hearty, loyal fondness for the theme, a truthfulness of description, which cannot fail to charm. It seems to say, with the perfumed earth in the Persian fable, "I am not the rose; but cherish me, for we have dwelt together;" and there is fragrance as of roses among its leaves. There can hardly be a treatise with less affectation and superfluity, so genuine, explicit, and natural, and so perfect a transcript of the man from whom it comes, that when I made his acquaintance, some years after my transformation, he exactly verified my expectations, and it was like meeting with an old and valued friend.

And thus I discovered, if not "books in the running brooks," a most fascinating volume in the Rivers of Hertfordshire, and in I plunged, as keen as Cassius (to Cæsar's unspeakable disgust), and as eagerly as a hot schoolboy taking "a header" into his favourite pool, truant it may be, and destined after his ablutions to the coarsest kind of towelling, but for the time as oblivious of all the ills which the fleshier part of youth is heir to, as though he bathed in Lethe. And just as this amphibious juvenile will emerge from time to time, and diversify his sport by a periodical canter in the flowery mead, so I quitted *my* Rivers at intervals, and wandering among my roses (I had but a dozen then) tendered my tardy but devoted allegiance. Or, as a pupil at Dotheboys Hall would be requested, after spelling the word "horse," to go and clean the quadruped in question, so I went from description to reality, first studying the portraits in my book of beauty, and then doing homage to those fair originals, born, or rather budded, so long to blush unseen, and waste their sweetness on my father's heir. How delighted I was, first to read, and then to have ocular proof, that Boula de Nanteuil was a "standard of excellence" (mine was only a half-standard, but let that pass); that Kean was "always beautiful, in size first-rate, and in shape perfection; that Coupe d'Hébé was "the gem of the family," and there, sure enough, I found her, a cup for the gods, and jewelled with dew-drops; and how disappointed I felt as I read that Madam Laffay "ought to be in every garden," but could not find her in mine, soon consoling myself, however, in the presence of Baronne Prevost and Duchess of Sutherland, and, on the whole, as well pleased with my new friends as was the author of my book when, one morning in June, looking over the first bed of roses he had ever raised from seed, he saw growing with great vigour one of the very very few good roses then originated in England, and subsequently called, perhaps because robust in habit as poor Brummel's "fat friend," Rivers's George the Fourth.

If this account of my resuscitation—if the suddenness with which I cracked the cocoon of my grubship and came out a rose-loving butterfly—appear to any of my hearers to be too severe a test of their implicit confidence in the narrator (in coarser English, "a corker "), I have testimony at hand to confirm my statements; and Mr. Evans is here, like the statue of Horatius, " to witness if I lie." He will readily recall his great astonishment when I first began to speak to him of flowers; how he smiled encouragingly upon me as a mother upon the baby just " beginning to take notice " (" bless it ! " exclaims mamma; " it's worth a million a minute ! " and nurse immediately follows with, " Yes, mum, two ! "); and how he would gaze upon me with an expression of kindly hope, as though he were some good physician, watching in his patient the first symptoms of recovery from delirious fever. He will recollect how rapidly our rosarium spread, since, as the poet of the seasons sings—

> " By swift degrees the love of nature works,
> And warms the bosom, till at last sublimed
> To rapture and enthusiastic heat,"—

until it finally invaded the kitchen-garden, and drove out the asparagus at the point of the digging-fork; and he will rejoice with me in remembering the time when our hostilities terminated; when Mars was to influence us no more, although that deity, according to Hesiod, was the son of a flower, and not of a gun, as one would be more disposed to imagine; when we turned our bayonets into pruning-knives, our swords into scythes, our mortars into garden-rollers, our helmets into flower-pots, our uniforms into shreds for the wall-trees, and our trumpet of war into a bird-tenter's horn.

You have seen a well-bred hunter turned out for his summer's run, when the soft showers of April have made the grasses green, and ere the suns of May, opening the buttercups, have converted every pasture into a Field of the Cloth of Gold. For half-a-dozen seconds, when the groom has quietly slipped over his nose the old "exercising bridle" which he knows so well, he stands gazing in amazement and perplexity, astonished as the rustic who, having formed his idea of cities from the occasional contemplation of a small market-town in the distance, sees for the first time from some commanding height great London spread out before him. Hardly, at first (I am referring to the horse), can he realize his freedom,—it seems to him too good to be true; but suddenly he apprehends the happiness of his state, and with a wild winny of delight he is away at speed, kicking as he goes, and giving ample demonstration to eye and ear that he thoroughly appreciates his new liberty. By-and-by he may condescend to a majestic trot, coming towards you with head erect, lithe, supple, elastic, "scarcely touching the ground, he's so proud and elate," and exhibiting a dignity and grace and power which you can see in no other animal, and only in him when thus unusually excited. After a while, perhaps, he may treat eye and nostril to a sight and scent of the young tender herbage; but he is much too happy to eat. Were he less so, he would hesitate where to begin, like the schoolboy whom you treat at the confectioner's, and bid, in Lear's words, "take all." But now he has youth's gladness without its appetite, and he is racing off again, head down and heels in the air, as though about to rehearse a series of somersaults for the edification of some favoured hippodrome.

A like joyous consternation, a like embarrassment of happiness are mine, my friends, when, released from the introductory part of my lecture, from my allegorical snaffle, I find myself free to expatiate upon a field—of roses, turned out as it were into the " rosea rura Velini," into those rose fields near Ghazepoor, which the great Bishop Heber tells us extended over many hundred acres, or into that " beautiful plain covered with innumerable roses," of which we read in the more recent " Wanderings of an Artist." So let me have a metaphorical gallop to relieve my exuberance of delight; or rather, since the rosarium is not good galloping ground, let me, like some nightingale just arrived in a rose nursery, and who can "scarce get out his notes for joy," take a preliminary fly over the premises, with obligato and irregular music, ere I settle down to sing in a more measured time and in a more usual key.

Hurrah, then, for the royal Rose! for a Queen who, like our own Victoria, reigns the wide world over in loving hearts! Hurrah for old England's emblem! emblem true of a happy land, whose sons flush quickly with a righteous anger to resent injustice and to defend the right, and whose daughters blush with a roseate beauty, with the "shame, which is a glory and a grace." Hurrah for the precious perfumed flower, which, for seven months of our fickle and inclement year, gives its welcome beauty to high and low, admired and loved by us all, from the patrician, who sees it in the golden epergne of the banquet, to the ploughboy, who sticks it in his coat o' Sundays, and seems to his younger brother, learning his collect, the embodiment of earthly bliss, as to a junior at Eton his gorgeous fraternity in the Life Guards! Hurrah for the flower, which in all history, sacred and secular, maintains priority of praise; which the Greeks named τὸ ἄνθος—*the* flower,—and of which all their poets, heroic, pastoral, sentimental, comic—Homer, Theocritus, Aristophanes, and "burning Sappho"— sang; which the Romans strewed before their victorious chiefs, chose first to ornament their homes and feasts, and even offered to their gods; which all nations, emancipated from barbarism, have ever fondly cherished; which displays its charms, as our English girls their loveliness, with an infinite variety of form, grace, and complexion, now *petite* as some pocket Venus (*Anglicè*, "a little duck"), and now beautiful abundantly—

"A daughter of the gods, divinely fair,
And most divinely tall"

(colloquially, "a glorious girl, sir"); which, only requiring in ordinary gardens the smallest share of attention to insure an ample bloom, may be induced by a patient and careful love to reveal its glories under adverse skies—which finally, my brothers, is the Queen of flowers, Rosa Mundi, perfect, peerless! "*Truie*," says the French proverb, "*truie aime mieux bran que roses*"—the sow would rather have its nose in the swill-tub than smelling the sweetest posy; and he is a hog who does not love the rose.

There! The hunter has had his gallop round the

"rosea rura," the nightingale alights breathless in his bower of roses; and we will moderate our pace now, if you please, and pitch our note an octave lower.

But we follow, though more slowly, the same route; the refrain of our song may not be changed, *Rose est Bonheur*, the rose is happiness!

For duration, in the next place, what flower dare upraise her head to dispute the supremacy of the rose? "Gather ye roses while ye may," says old Herrick; and with us rose-growers is it not almost "always *May*"? From that month to December—at all events, from the first blooms of the charming Banksiæ, of Gloire de Dijon, climbing Devoniensis and Maréchal Neil, on our warm south walls, until the last Giant of Battles must yield to Jack (the Giant-killer) Frost—we subjects of Queen Rosa may wear in our button-holes "of loyalty this token true." Whatsoever the weather in the intermediate months, however "deformed by sullen rains" or by continuous drought, a rose-tree, in good health to begin with, will have its bloom sooner or later; and, because different seasons suit different sorts, some trees in the rosarium will ever assume for our delectation their most perfect phase of beauty.

Consider, too, not only their diversity of colour—and if you wish for special examples of this compare Maréchal Neil with Duke of Edinburgh, or the Niphetos with Xavier Olibo—but also their diversity of form. You may grow the rose in a thumb-pot, with a flower "in shape no bigger than an agate-stone on the fore-finger of an alderman," or you may cover the front of your house with it. You may, in fact, grow the roses you most like in the form you most like—standards or half-standards, pillars, pyramids, or dwarfs. And I may say here, that I prefer to grow my own roses, generally speaking, on briers about two feet above the ground, for thus they require no unsightly props, no rain can spoil their blooms by beating them against the wet earth as with dwarfs—their complete beauty is brought at once before the eye, and, being within easy manipulation of the gardener, a symmetrical proportion is more readily attained, and of course more lastingly prolonged. Tea roses should be budded as low as possible on briers, grown from seed or cuttings, with a view to their protection from frost by mulching. Tall standards are very useful for the back row in borders, or as the centre of beds, but are rarely beautiful in an isolated state. Their most zealous admirers must allow, I think, that the more the brier is concealed the more attractive is the tree—that the more we see of the banner and the less we see of its pole the better; and no opponent of the standard, though he liked it as little as the brave Scots our standard at Northallerton, could require a more full confession.

Then, as to cost, you may establish a rose-garden with the money which is asked for a rare Pinus or Orchid, and may reproduce your favourite varieties on the brier or the Manetti, by the easy, interesting, and sure processes of budding or grafting, at a very small outlay, and to almost any extent. But be cautious, my Spades, unless you have a taste for rubbish, not to order your rose-trees, nor your anything else, from those cheap Jacks of the floral market, who profess to be so much more liberal than their neighbours. Buy good razors, O my friends, as ye love to enjoy your breakfasts with a temper smooth as your chin: and buy good rose-trees, O ye amateurs, as ye hope to look gladly on your feast of roses, when "the time of roses" shall come. The prices charged by the best growers are quite low enough (and you will believe one who has bought and buys largely) to insure a good article to the purchaser and a fair remuneration to the seller.

For ornamental purposes, as a cut flower, what have we so effective as the rose,—whether in the bouquet of some ball-room belle, herself—

> "A Rosebud set with little wilful thorns,
> And sweet as English air can make her,"—

in the elegant vases of the drawing-room, or, as I most rejoice to see them, in the cups of silver, won by their ancestors, upon the dinner-table and with the dessert? When Horace invites the friends of Plotius Numida to celebrate with appropriate honours the return of that distinguished officer from Spain, he bids them to have abundance of roses at their feast ("neu desint epulis rosæ"); and when he essays to "cheer up Sam," in the person of Q. Dellius, he recommends him to lose no time in giving an order for roses ("flores amœnos ferre jube rosæ"). Without endorsing his other recipes for driving dull care away, I may sympathise with him, I hope, in his love of the rose; and I like to fancy him, calling upon his friends to pass the Falernian, and, having previously proposed to them his favourite toast, "pulchræ puellæ, novies honorandæ" ("the Ladies, with three times three") requesting them to drink without heeltaps (the Latinity for heeltaps is lost*), "Vivat Regina Florum!" ("Long Bloom the Rose!").

I leave you, dear brothers, in their sweet society. Tend them with all love and care; and then, as surely as from the rose-trees of sunnier France comes the chief glory of our English gardens, you shall rejoice to repeat from a thankful heart,—"ROSE EST BONHEUR!"

CHAPTER VIII.

MR. OLDACRE'S STORY—THE LADY ALICE.

MR. PRESIDENT AND FRIENDS,—You must "pity the sorrows of a poor old man, whose trembling limbs," and here he glanced complacently at his well-filled gaiters, "have borne him to your" excellent gin-and-water, and must not look for anything remarkable in pippins from a decaying and exhausted apple-tree. As for lecturing you upon the culture of a garden, or haranguing you scientifically at all, I should no more think of it than of seeking horticultural information for myself in the books of those who wrote a century

---

* "Not so," writes a friend ("of Oxford he, a very learned clerk"); "the very word which precedes your quotation, namely, '*amystide*,' means to gulp down a bumper without closing the lips. Lucian also uses the word '$\alpha\mu\nu\sigma\tau\iota$.'"

ago on the subject; and I have no shame in the conviction, that some to whom I now speak, beginning at a point where I have all but stopped, and having opportunities and resources, developed since my manhood waned, know more about gardening than I do. It is sufficient for me to have been in my day with the foremost, and to have fought my way to many victories. But were I to "shoulder my crutch and show how fields were won" to you of this generation, or to manipulate my "Brown Bess," as an old musketeer, to you who have such an improved artillery as leads one to expect that England will soon be able to pepper her enemies, however distant, from batteries fixed upon her shores—to you who are blessed with a thousand facilities unknown to your ancestors, of smashing and ripping up your fellow-creatures—how would you forbear to smile? No; as old Mr. Whippy, the huntsman—or rather the ex-huntsman, for he has been, as you know, a pensioner for years of my noble master—trots after the hounds on his pony through the gaps and the gates, which he once despised, so must I now be content to look on from afar, travelling easily by quiet lanes and by-ways, and leaving the bravery and the honours of the chase to you.

So I will tell you, if you please, a simple story—a mere incident, in fact—which occurred many years ago in the family I serve, but which made at the time a great excitement among us, and may still, I hope, prove interesting to you.

Through the solemn avenue of cedars which leads to our mausoleum, I have followed three dukes to the grave. The second of these at one period of his life was most austere and haughty. I may speak of his faults, although he is dead, because he lived to hate them, and to cast them from him; and I have no hesitation in enlarging upon them, as the circumstances of my story prompt. Well, then, he was just the proudest, coldest, most disagreeable duke that ever stalked ("stalk, to walk with high and superb steps," says Dr. Johnson) over the earth. It was a positive insult to the English language to call so much ungraciousness "your grace." We gardeners used to declare that the thermometers fell twenty degrees whenever he walked through the houses; and that the water froze in the tanks and cisterns. We were prepared to affirm that when he put on his coronet the strawberry-leaves turned into ice-plants. Indeed, we all of us found a relief and comfort in this harmless kind of ridicule, just as schoolboys most delight to mimic the master who rules the most unkindly over them. It was a natural and pleasant rebound from the constraint and awful abasement to which his presence reduced us; and as for the propriety of our conduct, why, if men in high places are not high-minded, as they ought to be, they only become the more conspicuously assailable, and the homage which is offered to them is as unreal and worthless as the sham silver and the sham gold which the Chinese offer to their gods. So the duke played at being an idol, and we performed the worshipping. He thought himself something more than human, I am sure, and received our most lowly obeisance as though he were upon a golden throne.

His demeanour was calculated to give us the idea that we had no claim, strictly speaking, to existence in any form, but that he tolerated us. He sent for us, kept us waiting for hours, and then either dismissed us without an interview, or gave us his orders as though he gave out oakum to convicts. In my subordinate capacity I was only honoured with two brief conversations, during which he was pleased to address me, for he never remembered names, as " Mr. Cutts " and "Rowbottom,"—appellations which belonged respectively to the stud-groom and to an under-keeper, but which were as unlike Oldacre as, I daresay, he wished them to be.

We servants were not the only ones who shivered in his icy presence, and winked and capered with exuberant joy as soon as we were fairly out of it. Living at that time in one of the lodges, I frequently witnessed the arrival and departure of certain county families, who were annually distinguished by an invitation to the castle. To open the gate for these favoured guests, and to look upon their expression of complete despair, was like being hall-porter at a dentist's. They might have been blue-bottles, who had just set foot within the meshes of a spider's net, or rabbits, helplessly mesmerized by a weasel, and drawing nearer to their doom. One footman, I remember, was wont to weep in the rumble, and to assume for my edification such an aspect of pretended woe, pointing the while with his thumb to the unconscious tenantry of the chariot below, that at last I dared not go out to meet him, and he was compelled to dismount, and clear the way for himself.

But there was an entire change of performance, I can tell you, when these visitors came forth on their journey homeward; as distinct an alteration and improvement of countenance as may be observed in the features of that gentleman who appears from time to time in the pictorial advertisements, as now enduring the agonies of toothache, and now "Ha! ha! cured in an instant!" The tragedy, with its tyrant and dungeon-chains, was over; and, as the lamps blazed out once more, the orchestra, which had been executing Dead March and dirge underneath the darkened stage, emerged to play "Garry Owen." They who had come to us so silently and sadly, laughed and sang as they drove down the park. They could not have been in a happier frame of mind if they had been poachers coming out of jail in the shooting season. Hurrah! they were going home! home to have beer at dinner, and to turn to the fire at dessert! Home, to astonish the Browns, to fill the mouths of the Walkers with the waters of envy, and to awe the Bumbies with fancy statements about their "delightful visit at the castle." Well, I could bear truthful witness that the latter part of the proceeding had been delightful enough. As Robert Hall said to the pert young preacher, who asked what he thought of his sermon, "There was one very admirable passage —the passage from the pulpit to the vestry," so it might be affirmed with confidence that these guests had been especially happy in the last act and deed of —departure.

Now this iron duke, you will be surprised to hear, had actually condescended to marry. Of course, if

Cupid had not been blindfold, he would no more have thought of taking aim at him than a schoolboy of shooting his favourite arrow against the wall of a fives-court; and how that promiscuous young archer made his dart to stick in the ducal granite must remain for ever among the "things not generally known." Never since Eve had the world seen such a proof of love's omnipotence, as when he sent our grim lord a-courting. No weaker influence ever could have taught that cold, pale face to smile, to smile and to beam with a happy brightness, as the snow sparkles in the sun. But how he ever remembered her name, or brought himself to proffer those little tendernesses which are usual upon these occasions—those touches of nature which make the whole world kin—is to me a complete perplexity, an unreality as astonishing as though I were to see the ghost of Hamlet's father with his arm round the waist of Jessica.

Poor Jessica! she came to us as joyous as a thrush in summer, and she sang awhile blithely and sweetly in the tomb of Hamlet's father. But when he resumed, as he shortly did, his old sepulchral ways, a chill struck the heart of our singing-bird, and all her mirthful music was changed into a plaint and wail. She had come from a home of love and cheerfulness, and she drooped in his arctic atmosphere, as an orchid would drop in an ice-house.

> "For a trouble weighed upon her,
>   And perplexed her night and morn,
> With the burden of an honour,
>   Unto which she was not born."

Six years after her marriage-day they bore her slowly through the dark avenue of cedars, and the chaplain came in his white surplice to welcome her with words of hope and peace.

Three children were born to them. The marquis, who soon showed himself to be a true "chip of the old (ice) block," and a ghostling of amazing promise; Lord Evelyn and the Lady Alice, who, happily for us all, resembled their mother. Never were two brothers so unlike each other. I doubt whether the elder ever broke out of a walk or into a laugh in his life, whereas the younger would be scampering all over the place, with his little sister breathless behind, and his merry voice making our hearts glad. Now they were in the conservatory, changing the tallies, and sticking the falling flowers of the camellia upon the euphorbia's thorns; now turning out a lot of sparrows, which they had caught in traps, and adorned with appendages of brilliant worsted, red, green, and yellow, in the immediate neighbourhood of the aviary, and so essaying to impose upon us the idea of a general escape and dispersion of all our feathered curiosities; and now "drawing" the shrubberies, with Lord Evelyn at one end as master of fox-hounds (the foxhounds by an Irish retriever), and Lady Alice at the other as an under-whip, waiting, watchful and silent, for the fox to break, which he generally did in the guise of a blackbird; and then announcing his exit with the promptest and shrillest of "tally-hos." Our marquis the while was indoors at his books, having, it was reported, a precocious relish for algebra, and an insight into the science of political economy not often to be found (thank Heaven) in young gentlemen of fourteen.

Years passed. There was some misunderstanding between the marquis and the Cambridge examiners on the subject of his being Senior Wrangler, and the duke, after hearing his son's statement, was pleased to pronounce that the Dons were "offal." Lord Evelyn went into the Guards, and I shall never forget him on his first return from London, after an absence of six months from the castle. I was at tea in the lodge when his mail-phaeton drove up, and was hardly out of the porch, when his hearty "How are you, Oldacre?" drew my eyes to the handsomest, merriest, kindliest face that ever wore a moustache. And sitting by him was a brother officer, just the man you would have expected that my lord would choose for his friend, looking as though he would go at anything from an ox-fence to a redan, and yet would do no wilful hurt—as though his heart, like Tom Bowling's, was brave and yet soft; and he was, in the full beauty of its meaning, a gentle *man*. I went back to my wife, who had Frank Chiswick's wife, a baby, on her knee, and I said to her, "Susan, my lord's come, and has brought home a husband for Lady Alice." "I'll believe it," she answered, "when I see his wings! for the duke must have something more than mortal to suit him as a son-in-law."

And now, gentlemen, let the old horse catch his wind, if you please, dip his nose in the refreshing waters of the trough, and then trot on to the end of his journey.

The deer (said Mr. Oldacre, as he resumed his

story), having scampered away from the carriage-road, alarmed at the unusual sound of Lord Evelyn's merry laugh, had turned, and were still gazing in astonishment at the phaeton going up the park, when another equipage reached the entrance gates, containing two occupants, almost as upright, and quite as cold, as the pillars through which they passed. These were our noble marquis and a friend of his ("The Viscount," as he was afterwards called by us ; Lord Evelyn's friend being known as "The Captain"), very much resembling himself, both in the pallor of his countenance and in the haughty reserve of his demeanour. There they sat, straight and gloomy as a brace of Irish yews, which could not raise a berry —that is, a smile—between them.

I was reading the other day, in one of the books belonging to our "village library,"* for which we are mainly indebted to his reverence in the corner, how that the demeanour of King Philip II. of Spain, which was almost sepulchral, was ascribed partly to a natural haughtiness, and partly to habitual pains in the stomach, occasioned by an inordinate love of pastry. If the marquis and his friend were similarly affected, they must have recently paid a visit to the confectioner's, and stayed there until they had cleared the counter.

This solemnity of expression had probably been increased by the fact, which I afterwards heard from the postillions, that Lord Evelyn with his pair, had passed the marquis with his four, in jubilant derision

* Motley's " History of the Dutch Republic," vol. i.

and a hand-gallop not long before. If the latter had been drawn by four-and-twenty, the former would have gone by him just the same, for he always would be first. He had a sincere affection for his brother, but he delighted, as I have heard him say, "in cutting down old 'Quis," and when he had pounded him in a run, or bowled him in a match, he was happy. He was master in all sports, save one. The stern, imperturbable marquis was a dead shot. If all the pheasants, partridges, and wild ducks upon the estates to which he was heir, had arisen simultaneously, whirring and quacking around him, he would have selected his bird, and slain him as calmly as though there were but one. And he was never so solemnly fatal as when, after Lord Evelyn had fired hurriedly and harmlessly his right and left, he deliberately "wiped" the fraternal "eye." I used to load for my lord sometimes in covert shooting, when all available hands were pressed into the service; and I remember him saying to me on one occasion, as he handed me the smoking gun, "There's only one living thing in the world, Oldacre, which I thoroughly abhor and detest, and that's a beastly woodcock."

You begin to think, I fear, that I am "running to leaf," and therefore, although we gardeners have naturally a taste for garnish, I must prune accordingly. After a short visit, the marquis and Lord Evelyn went away with their friends; and rumours reached us from the servants' hall, that the latter had left a brace of hearts behind them, in custody of my Lady Alice. The duke, it was said, regarded with complete approbation the suit of the viscount, who was heir to an ancient and wealthy earldom; but the daughter preferred the Guardsman.

That there was some special attraction at the castle for these young gentlemen was evident from the fact that they both revisited it a few months after their departure, together with a great number of other guests, who were invited to celebrate the coming of age of our marquis. And now comes a chief event in my story. A grand ball was to end the festivities, and all the resources of our immense establishment were to be taxed to the utmost, as they say at the circus, to make the entertainment a success. We gardeners were busily engaged, I can assure you, in collecting and preparing all our eligible plants from the houses, carrying them to the castle, and arranging them in the halls, ballroom, &c. The demand for cut flowers, upon the day of the ball, was (so my father, then the head-gardener, pronounced it) murderous; flowers for the reception-rooms, flowers for the supper-table, flowers for the hair, flowers for the hand, and flowers for the gentlemen's coats.

As I was at that time head foreman in the plant department, the care of the great conservatory was entrusted to me during the night of the ball. I was to replace any of the low flowering plants, which formed an edging to the circular beds, and which might be disarranged by the trailing garments of the ladies; to supervise the fountains, which were at times eccentric in their behaviour; to keep an eye upon the coloured lamps, &c. When the guests came into the conservatory, I was to retire behind a stage for plants at the end of the building, where I should be effectively concealed within my leafy bower.

Here, without any attempt or desire to listen, I overheard from time to time the remarks of those who were passing near, and I was specially impressed by the floral instruction which I received for the first time on that occasion. One gentleman informed his partner that the berries of the Solanum were "a kind of Siberian crab;" another, that the tulip, Rex rubrorum, was "a double poppy;" a third, that Eucharis amazonica was "one of those lovely orchids;" and a fourth (a lady) exclaimed in admiration, as she gazed upon a bush of Cytisus, "What a dear little duck of a young laburnum!" But there were other flowers that night, which, even in Flora's presence, were more admired than ours—heart's-ease and forget-me-nots in the blue eyes of Beauty, roses blushing and glowing on her cheeks, lilies and tulips upon her—

"Hands, lily-white,
Lips, crimson-red,"

much more fascinating than those which we showed in pots. In foliage we sustained a like defeat. They turned from our Croton angustifolium to the shining tresses of some Fair One with the Golden Locks, and they saw no charms in our Adiantums, when compared with the maiden-hair of Venus' self.

The ball was nearly over. The carriage-lamps of the departing guests were gleaming amid our ancient oaks, as though some of the planets had come down to earth, and my own special lamps, within their bright pictorial cases, were also beginning to take their departure, when, as I retired to my ambuscade, on hearing voices, the Guardsman, with Lady Alice on his arm, approached, and stopped close in front of it. I saw them through the leaves, the handsomest man and the most beautiful woman of all who met there that night. It was not only that they were both tall and graceful in figure, with features regular and refined, the eyes bright, and the cheeks glowing with all the healthfulness and hopefulness of youth; but there was in both faces that which I would term heart-beauty; there was goodness, gentleness, and truth. And yet, as "these two, a maiden and a youth, stood there, gazing," or seeming to gaze, upon an orange-tree covered with its blossoms, I noticed upon both the expression of a strange and sad perplexity. For a while they were silent, and then the soldier said, "I am going in a few hours: I must speak to you. Would you—would you exchange *those*" (and he looked at the roses in her bouquet); "would you change them for *these*" (and he touched one of the orange-flowers)—for my sake—for me?"

I shall never forget that beseeching voice. It thrilled me through with the anxiety which it expressed, and I leaned forward to hear the answer. "I—I—I believe that I am engaged to the viscount." Then for a few awful seconds there might have been in that conservatory no living soul, for there was no sound save of distant music, faintly heard from the ball. At last he spoke with a great effort,—"I have no right to ask you; but do you love him?" And she, in a tone which cut my heart like a knife, replied, "My father, the duke, wishes me to marry him." "Not," he said passionately, "if you do not love him!" and then there was another dreadful silence, broken by these hopeless, whispered words, "I cannot, I dare not, disobey the duke. Some one is coming; we must go."

I do not think that the Guardsman knew quite what he was doing, but what he did was this: he plucked a leaf from the orange-tree, and gave it to her, and said, "If ever there is hope for me, or I can help you, send me this leaf."

Then others joined them, and they went their way. I stayed there, mute and motionless, thinking what cruel tyranny it was to crush those young loving hearts, until a footman came to say that the ball was over; and then I hurried home, weary and sorrowful; and I remember that before I went to bed that night, I prayed that she might send him the leaf. But Mrs. Oldacre, from whom I never had a secret, declined to regard the circumstances as becoming subjects for doubt or petition. She sniffed at my solicitude with a grand disdain, "because I *know*," she said, "that she will send it to him."

Of course we kept the secret sacredly; but Phyllis, my wife's sister, and maid to the Lady Alice, seemed to us to know as much as we did. She was ever sounding the captain's praise, or speaking of his rival in anything but respectful terms, alluding to him as "that galvanized mummy," and expressing her belief that he had been placed as a boy in a petrifying well, and been imprudently taken out before the process was complete. "And though I dare not speak my mind to his lordship," she said, "I have had the pleasure of telling his valet that we don't intend to marry a snow man."

Nevertheless, we heard to our great unhappiness that the wedding-day was fixed. The announcement was painful to most of us, but it seemed to have the strongest and the strangest influence upon our sister Phyllis. She would no longer speak of that which had been her one topic of conversation. She had a nervous manner and an anxious look. Sometimes she would laugh almost hysterically; and sometimes, my wife told me, she would come to her in a paroxysm of grief and tears, for which she would assign no cause.

Then another strange incident happened to me. The evening before our annual county flower-show I had been occupied until it was almost dark, in tying and packing a collection of stove and greenhouse plants, which I was going to exhibit, when, in taking a short cut from the kitchen-gardens across the park to my home, and passing over the long walk, which is a continuation, as you know, of the grand terrace, and extends for nearly a mile through our woodland grounds, I saw, ten yards from me, but in such earnest conversation that they never heard my steps, two figures, and, dim as the light was, I was quite certain that I knew them. I almost ran the rest of my way, and, in a fever of excitement, I whispered to my wife, "Lady Alice has sent him the leaf."

She received my information not only with disbelief but derision, and next day she sent for her sister Phyllis, to assist her in disbelieving. They said it was simply impossible; that it was one of the house-maids and the under-whip; that Lady Alice was in bed with the toothache (oh, Phyllis, Phyllis!), and that the captain was in Windsor barracks. And when I suggested that as I was there, with a brace of eyes in good working order, and they were not, I must respectfully take leave to differ; then they said, that if I had seen anything, which they did not for a moment believe, I ought to be ashamed of myself spying into people's houses (half a mile off) at that time of night, intruding into private walks, &c. I could only plead that up to that hour I had not been aware that after nightfall the duke's park was solemnly given up to the young nobility, paired off, and dying for love.

Finally, after reiterating for the (as nearly as I can guess) forty-second time, that I had seen nothing, they implored, they insisted, that I should never reveal to living creature that which I had seen; and I gave them at last my promise to keep a secret, which nothing upon earth could have tempted me to tell.

* * * * *

The marriage morning came. On the day preceding I had decorated the church as sorrowfully almost as though it had been for her funeral, and at sunrise I had arranged a bouquet (it was composed of stephanotis, pancratium, gardenia, and white rosebuds) which I had mourned over as if for her coffin. "And so," I sighed to myself, "the leaf went, and the lover came; and yet there was neither help nor hope."

The events of the day, as we ascertained afterwards,

were these: you will see that they require no commentary.

The party at the castle was to assemble in the library at 11 a.m.; to leave the castle at 11.15, and to meet the viscount at the church.

At 9 a.m., Lady Alice's favourite cousin, and chief bridesmaid, went to see her, and was met at her dressing-room door by Phyllis, who told the young lady that her mistress had passed a restless night and had just fallen asleep.

At 10 a.m., on a second visit, the cousin was informed by the maid that Lady Alice would rather not see any one until she came down for the marriage.

At 11 a.m., the guests, with the family, met in the library.

At 11.15, a dozen carriages, three of them having four horses, and two with outriders, drew up in front of the castle.

At 11.25, the duke sent a servant to inform the Lady Alice that he hoped she would come down at once.

At 11.35, the servant returned to inform the duke that "*her ladyship was not to be found!*"

Then the duke calmly requested that her ladyship's maid should be sent to him in his morning-room.

And, after a long interval, the report was brought to him, that "*her ladyship's maid was not to be found!*"

Then some one discovered, on Lady Alice's writing-table, a note to her father, the duke. It was, so Phyllis informed us, to this effect: that she had pleaded in vain that she did not love the viscount—

that it could not be right that her whole life should be turned into a lie—that it should be a life of hatred when it might be a life of love—that she was gone with him who had won her heart, to be his wife—and that she implored her father to forgive her for her mother's sake.

The duke turned very pale, and the duke sighed very heavily, when he had read the note, as well, with his views, he might. His only daughter was travelling as fast as four horses could take her, and had been travelling for six hours as fast as four horses could take her, to marry a younger son.

Then his grace wrote a few lines to the viscount, who was waiting for his bride.

> "The kirk was decked at morning-tide,
> The tapers glimmered fair;
> The priest and bridegroom wait the bride,
> And dame and knight are there.
> They sought her baith by bower and ha'—
> The ladie was not seen!
> She's o'er the Border, and awa'
> Wi' Jock of Hazeldean."

And once "o'er the Border" (I may as well state here), they were married in conformity with Scotland's usage, that they might be man and wife, should pursuers overtake, according to secular law; and subsequently, that they might be so according to the laws of their Church and conscience, by an ordained priest.

Three hours after the viscount had read his note, all the visitors had left the castle; and in it and around " grim silence held her solitary reign." The only person who passed through *our* entrance gates with a cheerful countenance (my wife informed me) was my Lord Evelyn. He was just as beaming with mirth and kindness as ever. "Sad business," he said, "Mrs. Oldacre; bad business—disgraceful business," with a broad grin on his face. And then he began to sing something (Mrs. O. continued) about a way they had in the army, or words to that effect.

Yes, they all fled from that stern and stricken duke, as though they were seized with a sudden fear that he was going to bark and bite them. True indeed it was, that then, and for many after-days, his grace was not good company. He was seen only by those who waited upon him, and their report of his melancholy was very pitiful. What, think you, happened next?

My friends (said the good old gardener, with tears in his kind blue eyes), it pleased God in His goodness, by that great humiliation, to change, and, as I believe, to save one of His creatures. Some three weeks after the crisis, the duke left the castle for the first time, and went to the mausoleum. He remained there so long that some of the household were beginning to be alarmed, when he came quietly home, and sent a note to his chaplain, with whom shortly afterwards he had a two hours' interview. We have always thought that he made then a first and full confession. He was from that time, at all events, an altered man. He sent not only his pardon to his daughter, but a fatherly invitation to her old home; and she came with her husband, and with gladness for all our hearts.

This reconciliation, the first fruit of that victory which he had won over self, soon brought its great reward, partly in the fact that the handsome Guardsman succeeded, against all expectation, to the headship of his house—a peerage, with large estates—but chiefly in his daughter's grateful love.

We will leave him, if you please, as I once saw him, and as ever since I have liked best to think of him, plucking an orange for his grandchild, little Alice, *from the very tree whereupon grew the leaf.*

CHAPTER IX.

MR. CHISWICK ON BEDDING-OUT.

GENTLEMEN,—Æsop does not tell us whether thirteen respectable frogs held a coroner's quest over the remains (which must have been collected and arranged with difficulty) of that ambitious brother who, foolishly essaying to represent to his family the grand proportions of the ox, induced a sudden disruption of the cuticle, or, in the vulgar parlance, *bust*. If such an inquiry was made, and the frogs, our esteemed progenitors according to the Darwinian theory, may probably have enjoyed, as we do, the rich blessing of trial by jury, they could only have anticipated the verdict which the colliers in a wild mining district pronounced more recently upon a terrible virago who had fallen down a shaft, with the assistance of her husband—to wit, that it "served her right." Although the bereaved family—the brothers and sisters, for anything we know to the contrary, of the ill-fated flirt who perished so suddenly in the bloom of his youth and in his opera hat—had pleaded with tears for a verdict of ranicide, and a big deodand on the ox, no honest frog could have forgotten for a moment the plain demands of duty.

And yet, my brother Spades, it has been not seldom affirmed in my hearing by several horticultural frogs, who have burst themselves—that is to say, have completely ruined their gardens by extravagant efforts to reproduce, for their neighbours' astonishment, the outlines of a certain modern ox, known to us by the name of "Bedding-Out"—that their dissolution was murder, and not suicide. "See," they have cried in the crisis of evisceration, in their anything but happy despatch, "how this detestable monster has ruined our little plot, broken down our flowering-shrubs, crushed our herbaceous plants, and left us nothing, in place of our sweet unfailing beauty, but a brief and scentless glare!" The very men who hacked down and uprooted their laburnums and lilacs, and weigelas and pyrus, and berberis and ribes, with all the energy and exultation of backwoodsmen, who sentenced their old herbaceous favourites to transportation for life, and rejoiced to consign them, packed like convicts in crowded wheel-barrows, to penal settlements in the kitchen-garden—I have heard them, and so have you, plaintively protesting against their own free act and deed, as though it had been done at point of bayonet, and as though every hesitation and entreaty of theirs had only been answered by an extra *prod*. The fact is, that in this matter of bedding-out, a large number of our brotherhood have felt, with good reason, ashamed of themselves—ashamed of having sacrificed and slighted so much that is beautiful, from a foolish ambition, which they could never realize, to produce sensational effects, and, like naughty dogs, who deserve but dislike castigation, they will creep through any hole in the fence to keep out of range of the whip.

I mean, in plainer English, that the system of bedding-out is a grand discovery, a charming ornamentation and additional grace where it can be appropriately introduced and amply provided for; where it can be well done in a suitable site, and where it comes, without trespass or ejection, as an ally and not as an opponent; but that in a small garden, where it destroys, or even interrupts the natural succession of hardy plants and shrubs, it is a very sad mistake—a mistake which, by abusing and misapplying a beautiful branch of horticulture, has brought it into disrepute.

Where shall we find, for example, a more pleasing conformity than in the tasteful bedding-out of those terrace gardens which surround so many of our great castles and mansions, and in which architecture and horticulture are combined in such graceful unison; the stone walls and balustrades, and edgings of the beds, contrasting so effectively with the bright colours of leaf and flower? and this, moreover, for eight months in the year, from March to October, if the gardener be an artist, with means and with men to realize his art, and to maintain in continuous beauty that bright mosaic basement.

What, on the other hand, more dreary or wasteful

than a small garden, treeless and flowerless for two-thirds of the year? A garden, did I say?—a grass plot the rather, diversified by patches of bare brown earth, the work, it might be, of a school of moles who were studying geometry beneath.

I may be asked here, why assign eight months of beauty to the garden on the rich man's terrace, and only four to the garden on the poor man's lawn? The answer is, because when the garden is small, the resources, as a rule, will be small also, restricting the supply to those plants which flower during the summer months. Bedded out in May, these will attain their charms in July, and retain them probably for the period named. But where the material is unlimited and the culture skilled, the spring flowers will be gay in March; and on their removal, the introduction of blooming and foliage plants, more advanced than those which are grown where glass is less abundant, will produce an immediate and effective display.

And chiefly, I would protest against the exclusive appropriation of a small garden to that which may be termed the summer system, not only because it brings with it the miserable nakedness, the long, dreary, dirty desolation, to which I have referred, but withal a result yet more deplorable. It destroys the sentiment, the teaching, the associations, the memories, and the hopes, of which a garden should be the haunt and home. Great poets have written tender poesy upon the brightness and sweetness, the grace and the peace, of a garden, as it used to be. They rejoiced to watch, here in cool grot, or there from the sunny walk, the natural development of its beauty—from the first snowdrop in spring to the last rose of summer, so varied, so ample, and so sure. They sang, like the birds, heart-music, from its fragrant bowers; but who has sung or can sing in or concerning those treeless, shrubless, exposed and shadeless squares, to which the blackbird comes only for his worm, and flies to seek in some more favoured garden a twig on which to chant his grace? The Muse can only weep and wail, because the Muse must be aware that Flora, whom she loves, is here but decked and exhibited to catch the public eye, and behind the scenes she is starved and beaten. The Muse is aware that for a considerable portion of the year herbaceous ghosts, arboric apparitions, and bulbous bogies, haunt this now gaudy ground. She is not to be deceived, my brother, no more than you or I when we see some silly wench on a Sunday with half a year's wages on her back, and a month's ditto on her shining hair, as full of oil as a salad, and know that to-morrow she will be a slipshod sloven, indolent, morose, and grimy.

Denouncing the summer system, where it has a monopoly, as destructive of sentiment and of amiable associations, let me tell you an incident which happened within my observance, and which condemned it in my eyes, and in the eyes of one yet more nearly interested, as the desecration of an English home. Some years ago I held the situation of under-gardener at a country place, where an old-fashioned garden, full of beautiful shrubs and plants, was suddenly sacrificed to the fashion of the day and the bad taste of the owner, cleared, levelled, laid out in an elaborate design, and dedicated to the summer system. In the following year, a sailor-son of the family, who had been at sea as a midshipman, came back from his voyage, and soon after his arrival was brought into the garden to see the "improvement." I happened to be there at work; and as the beds were very gay, and glowing with scarlet, purple, and gold, I expected to hear great admiration. Only a sigh came from his lips, and I saw in his face a sore distress. Afterwards he came to me, and confided, for we were mates in the cricket-field, and I had carried his landing-net many a time: "Frank, I couldn't have believed that they could have shaved, and hacked, and tattooed, and daubed the dear old place like this. I loved every tree and shrub in it, and I've dreamed of them, and been looking for nests, and playing hide-and-seek among them, a thousand miles away, with nothing but salt water all around. Why, they have taken away the very fuchsia which I saw poor Mary" (his dead sister) " plant!"

And now I have only to repeat, before I speak of "Bedding-Out" descriptively, that, while I denounce the system in its exclusive usurpation of the garden, and shall presently denounce it in another phase as a failure and imposition, I heartily admire it, carefully treated, as an auxiliary grace and gain; nor would I restrict its application to the grand terraces and the extensive grounds of which I have before spoken. If I may suggest to you a rule for our guidance, it is this — wherever there is a goodly supply of the best hardy shrubs and plants, and space to spare, there let us have the bedding-out system, providing always that this space shall be occupied not only in summer but in spring. No part of a flower-garden should consist of brown earth during those eight months of the year in which our climate permits, and we gardeners can provide, a covering of flower and leaf.

There are three seasons and three systems of bedding-out, the winter, the spring, and the summer.

If we regard winter bedding-out under the most auspicious circumstances, when the atmosphere exhilarates, and our digestion is good, and our debts are few, we may possibly derive from it about as much amusement as from a third or fourth-rate farce; but if we criticise it severely after unpleasant letters, or a pill, or when the wind is in the east, we can only speak of it as the Attorney-General spoke of the Tichborne Claimant, and denounce it as an impostor, a humbug, and a sham. Beds of baby evergreens, new-born hollies, infant aucubas, tiny junipers, and the like, edged with variegated ivies, arabis, &c., with most of the variegation washed and frozen out of them—these, as they peep out of the snow like a lot of black pins in a white pincushion, evoke the gardener's ire, not only as an insult to his art, but as the abortive attempt of an insatiate greediness to get more than generous Nature will give. For my own part, I can only think of two exceptional cases in which these feeble failures, dignified by the name of winter bedding-out, might be benevolently excused. They might be introduced into the garden of a retired nurseryman, superannuated and in his dotage, as soothing reminiscences of early life; or mamma might have a bed of them in front of the nursery window, and point to them, when reading the voyages of Gulliver, as charming illustrations of the forest scenery of Liliput. "They be for children," as Lord Bacon said of yew-trees clipped into dolphins and peacocks; and I remember an instance in which children made a striking and serio-comic use of them.

I was contemplating the only attempt which I ever made to realize the meek, modest, little idea of transforming winter into summer, and of breaking in the garden committed to my charge the annual Sabbath of its rest—and I was thinking what a dreary disappointment it was, when my attention was drawn to the altered appearance of a bed, in which a large number of juvenile Irish yews were arranged with a dreadful uniformity. Little mounds had been raised here and there among them, and a large white wooden "tally," taken from the potting-shed, was inserted at the head of each. On a closer scrutiny, the beak of a defunct robin was observable rising out of one of these small hillocks, while from another the corpse of an ancient doll exhibited its toeless foot; and my conjecture as to the meaning and intention of these arrangements was speedily verified by a sweet little voice, which said, "Oh, please, Mr. Tissick, me, and Blanche, and Bertie have been playing at Cementerry, and Victoria Eugenie would not go into her coffin" (a cigar-box), "and Bertie went and got his night-gown, and was going, you know, to be a clergyman, but Blanche said pa would not like it, and so we gave it up."*

And I also gave up playing at Spring. I saw that Winter, like an honest, handsome old gentleman, disdained to dye his silvery beard and to act the dandy with a flower in his coat. I broke up my exhibition of dwarfs and pigmies, and distributed them in the shrubberies and borders. I parted with my magnificent collection of chromo-lithographs— that is to say, I removed in a wheel-barrow my walks, composed of coloured stones and shells, of brick-dust, tile-dust, coal-dust, cockles, gypsum, and other

---

* Here I must tell a couple of authentic histories concerning dolls, in the belief that they will amuse the British public as they amused me. A six-year-old child, the son of the village schoolmaster, left his mother's side during the baptism of an infant in the church here, and had made some progress towards the font, when he was missed, pursued, and captured. Subsequently questioned as to his motive, he produced from his pockets two very dirty dolls, negroes in complexion and in scant costume also, and informed his parents, "He was going to take 'em to Mister Rennunds" (during my father's lifetime I was known in the parish as "Mr. Reynolds") "to be tistened." Anecdote No. 2 is this :—Two wee lassies, aged five and six, were playing in a room with their dolls, and their mother, at her writing-desk, was listening to their talk. The dolls were taken to various imaginary entertainments, walks, rides, drives, visits, and parties, and at last they were taken to church. "Now, dear, will you sit in this pew?" said one ; "and will you, dear, sit in this pew?" said the other. Whereupon the mother saw an opportunity of improving the occasion, and interposed with the remark, "We don't have pews, you know, in our church ; the seats are free and open to all, because all are equal there." And one of the little playmates immediately looked up and said, "Oh, yes, dear ma; but just now we're playing at very Low Church indeed ! "

cheerful rubbish. If, I asked myself, we once admit this tea-garden trumpery, where are we to stop? I have seen, in the grounds of a suburban drinking-house, an Araucaria imbricata done in cast-iron, and painted appropriately a bottle-green. What if the idea should spread? What if somebody, with "no end of tin" and no beginning of taste, should "go in," regardless of expense, for a metallic winter garden, electro-plated Silver Hollies, Gold-leaf Yews, and real Copper Beeches? Why limit the collection to hardy shrubs and trees? Why not a Battersea Park at Christmas? Why not all the beautiful foliage of the stove? Why not Alocasia metallica in real bronze? Nay, why foliage only? Why not flowers and fruits? Why not purple grapes, and blushing peaches, and all the glowing splendour of August, defying 20° of frost?

Seriously, there is but one legitimate winter garden, and that, no doubt, an enjoyable luxury to those who can afford it—I mean, under glass. But why should we crave it? Though we had neither greenhouse nor stove, we might be well content to rest with our plants and trees; to rest and be thankful for the past, to rest and be hopeful for the future. Some, of course, will say, "Ye are idle, ye are idle. You gardeners are always resting on your spades, always sitting under your vines and fig-trees, instead of pruning and thinning." We need not make answer for ourselves. All who possess a garden and know anything about it, know this also, that never in the history of horticulture was so much required, and so much realized from the gardener.

For example, and to pass to the second part of my lecture, there is Spring bedding-out, in my eyes by far the most attractive feature of modern horticulture. The most beautiful because the most natural, gladdening our hearts with a new happiness and with new hopes, just when Nature herself awakes in

> "The delicious trouble of the spring,"

when the sap is rising in the branches on which the thrushes sing, and the child finds the first violet—blue-eyed and sweet as childhood itself—upon the sunny southern bank, or comes tottering into the broad green woodland "ride," holding up a primrose in its tiny fist triumphantly, as one to whom had just been given the first prize for a hand-bouquet. Then it is that the gardener's art,—the art

> "Which does mend Nature; change it rather: but
> The art itself is Nature,"—

changes and mends most successfully that which the first gardener marred and disfigured, because it is then most in union with Nature, assisting, developing, obeying, copying, as a loving, reverent disciple, and not dictating nor innovating, as a proud omniscient lord. In a spring garden we "change and mend" only by multiplication, and by such improvement, or rather restoration, as vigilant care and cultural art can give. All our charming varieties of Viola, and Primula, and Myosotis, and Anemone, and Erica, for example, are collected and cherished there, when the first primrose and violet (as I have said), the forget-me-not, and wild-flower, and wild heath, come forth in their season, upon bank and mountain, in their woodland and moorland homes. The wild bulbs in their habitations (what time the Nottingham meadows are empurpled by their crocus bloom) break forth into beauty with ours. The flowers in a spring garden look at home and happy. They know, as old friends, that they are welcome, and they smile their thanks. They are not as dainty and magnificent swells, who have been delicately nurtured (under glass), who seem too grand for their surroundings, and who will leave us, if foul weather come.

Then consider the diversity of colour, form, and combination which is found among these vernal flowers. Let us imagine that the winter is past, and that we survey their bright charms once more. Let us ask the beneficent fairy, who changed a pumpkin into a chariot to convey Cinderella to the ball, to transform one of those huge gourds which adorn our club-room into an omnibus, and bid Fancy drive us to —Spring Gardens.

Arriving, we shall be as surprised and delighted as Cinderella herself, —

> "When tapers shone,
> And music breathed,
> And beauty led the ball."

Surprised! Why, there is not one in a thousand, even of those who love a garden—nay, there is not one in a hundred of my brother gardeners, who knows the marvellous charms of a spring garden extensively and tastefully arranged; and, had I power and permission, nothing would please me more than to act as a sort of horticultural Mr. Cook, of unbounded benevolence and wealth, to superintend gratuitous excursions of the floral fraternity to Belvoir, Cliveden, Wardie Lodge, and elsewhere, from the middle of March to the end of April. Our vernal flowers have gone gradually, but in many cases entirely, from our gardens. His reverence told us, a few Sundays ago, that people nowadays were quite as fond of telling and hearing new things as ever they were at Athens when St. Paul was there; and this love of novelty and display has been at work in our guild, and induced us to despise and discard the fair and faithful favourites of the past.

Two of the songs with which our old friend Mr. Grundy has occasionally entertained us always remind me of our disgraceful and perfidious misconduct, as gardeners, with reference to hardy flowers. In his "Labourer's Song," one rustic complains to another,—

> "Folks thinks still
> Nowt's good now as used to was,
> My owd friend Bill."

And there has been a sad season, not long past, in horticulture, in which few cared for that which all could have, and all things old were vile. In another melody he tells us how the proud ploughboy, on his promotion, cruelly cuts his former friends:—

> "And little Nell, I loved so well,
> And walked so wi' o' Sundays,

Good lor, says I, don't talk to me,
Ise mon at Mestur Grundy's!"

So, I fear, it has been in many cases with the gardener. He was promoted to serve in houses of glass; he was introduced to gorgeous company; he was wooed by a more brilliant and aggressive beauty; and he forgot, as he gazed upon such dazzling charms, the sweet little modest maiden whom once he "loved so well."

But again I say "surprised," for who can pass from the external gloominess of an English March, the leafless hedges, the brown fallows, the slaty clouds, the flowerless gardens, into a scene of the liveliest, loveliest beauty, and not feel surprise? And delight! such a sudden and sweet refreshment! I remember, when I lived near London, being in a crowded omnibus one sultry summer's day in the Strand, with the large mother of a thirsty babe on the one side, and a German Jew, who had not been smoking the sort of tobacco which I like, on the other. I was feeling about as comfortable as a white camellia in a coal-pit, and was literally gasping for breath, when the omnibus, having made an unusual progress of nearly eighty yards, drew up just opposite one of those narrow streets which lead from the great thoroughfare to the Thames, and a cool, fresh, delicious breeze from the river blew upon my brow! Such a revival to the floral spirit is the first sight of the flowers of spring.

Recall the charming diversity of colour and of form which they, the annuals, perennials, and bulbous plants of spring, present to our admiration. Of form, from the tall imperial fritillaria, having the resemblance of crown and of sceptre also, to the prostrate stonecrop, carpeting the ground beneath. Of colour, what a range, what a rich variety! All colours, primary and intermediate, brilliant and soft, positive and neutral—colours to harmonize, colours to contrast, the colours which I like, and the colours which you like—all of them are here. Does your eye delight in the glow and brightness of the more vivid tints? Look at that anemone, well-named "fulgens," all afire in crimson glory! Regard these tulips—General Garibaldi, in his scarlet uniform, or royally named and royally apparelled, rex rubrorum, the King of the Reds! Gaze upon that gentian (the vernal), luminous, gleaming like the breast of a humming-bird with an intense and dazzling blue! Watch that clump of the yellow crocus, as they open to receive the kisses of the sun (if any); and what is there in the stove, or even in the summer-garden, in orchid, allamanda, or calceolaria, which can vie with them in their golden sheen?

Or have you what is called a more "quiet taste"? Bend over this bed of myosotis dissitiflora, bluer than the turquoise, blue as the heavens, and you need not ask from the gardener, or search in floral dictionary, a translation of the name, for the flower itself speaks it in your ear, and whispers, "forget-me-not." Or turn to that patch of the exquisite, dainty little scillas ("from the Scilly Islands," I once heard a gentleman, who set up to be a wit, remark to a lady, who promptly set him down by replying,

"Did you come over in the same ship?"), or to that sheet of roseate silene, blue mountain-anemone, purple pansy, pale yellow primrose, bright yellow cheiranthus, lilac aubrietia, or (yet more appropriate to one who is talking of sheets) to those snow-white masses of candytuft (iberis correæfolia is the fairest of the fair), of alyssum, arabis, saxifrage, daisy, and snowdrop.

Now glance at the combinations: at that bed of golden feverfew, dotted here and there with the purple crocus; of white candytuft, from which at intervals the bright red hyacinths rise; or of cerastium, with small circular patches of scarlet anemone or Cliveden pansy, or of erica carnea, with the golden arabis intermixed; or of sedum acre aureum, with white and red tulips inserted à la pincushion. Would you have something more striking and effective even than these? Copy two beds, which I first saw at Belvoir and shall never forget; the one of

"Daffodils,
Which come before the swallow dares, and take
The winds of March with beauty,"

intermixed with purple hyacinths; and the other of aucuba japonica, which was blended with the many-coloured kale. So impressed was I with the latter combination, that Mr. Ingram, a gardener worthy of that princely place, and one who, like the castle by which he dwells, "hath a pleasant air," and, like a true artist, a kind brotherly sympathy with all who love his art, noticed my interest, and gave me some seed. This was sown at once, came up, was transplanted, and finally placed, in the autumn, in a bright bed of healthy young Aucubas, selected for the purpose. Alas, alas! one moonlight February night, *that* footman, whom I never could admire, although his calves were grand, left the gate between the park and the pleasure-ground open; and when I went to take a last look at my fires, the cattle were on my flower-beds chewing their cuds, and their cuds were composed of my variegated kale, which they had brutishly mistaken for cow-cabbage!

I have no time to speak of harmonies and gradations in colour, of rings, ribbons, pyramids, and baskets; but I must say a few words about foliage, because I have heard some folks, who should know better, say that, prate as we may about spring flowers, we can speak nothing in praise of spring foliage. No praise! Why, after admitting a defeat in the darker leafage and sounding a retreat on our creeping bugle (ajuga reptans) before the coleus, amaranthus, iresine, and beet; and after a further concession that we have no single leaf so beautiful as Mrs. Pollock,—we advance our whole army for a general engagement, with no fear of the result, and, in the poetical words of Transatlantic fervour, " we pounds the univarse smart." What foliage is so attractive in the summer-garden as that of the gold-tipped stonecrop (sedum acre aureum), of the daisy, which has leaflets of green and gold (bellis aucubæfolia), or of the exquisite variegated thyme? Is not the golden feverfew brightest in spring? Are not the variegated arabis, euonymus, and periwinkle, the silvery cerastium, centaurea, gnaphalium, and santolina, most beautiful in their early growth? When is the dactylis, or our old friend the gardener's garter, so silvery or so graceful as in spring? Stoop now to admire this variegation of white and of gold in lamium maculatum aureum, of green and silver in that charming spiræa. And now regard the manifold varieties of "that rare old plant, the ivy green," forming such a natural floor or cincture for the smiling splendour of the spring!

And all the while, what fragrance from violet and primrose, from hyacinth and wallflower,* from daphne, mezereon, and thyme! Mr. Ingram plants large beds of his Russian violets near the entrance-gate of the Belvoir garden, to breathe a welcome to the visitor; but from all parts of it sweet incense rises heavenward.

I have said nothing of the flowering trees and flowering shrubs, which should form a part of all spring gardens, surrounding them, and here and there forming centres for the beds; the blossoming fruit-trees, peach, almond, and cherry; the laburnums and syringas, the rhododendrons and azaleas, the weigelas, ribes, and berberries. I have passed over hundreds of bonny winsome flowers. Volumes might be written, volumes have been written, about them; and to two of these I would especially refer those readers who desire the best information, namely, to Mr. William Robinson's book upon Hardy Flowers, and to Mr. David Thomson's "Handy Book of the Flower-Garden."

* "Very delightful," as Lord Bacon says, "to be set under a parlour or lower chamber window."

There yet remains to be mentioned, and that with thankful praise, the most gracious and precious attribute of these bright vernal flowers—they can be multiplied quickly and abundantly, and they scarcely need any cultural care. Many of them cover the ground with wonderful rapidity, and send out roots as they spread. Thus they are propagated readily by division, and most of them by cuttings and by seed also. They are just as beautiful and enjoyable in single plants by the cottage-door as in masses nigh the mansions of the rich. Like all the best gifts of our merciful Father, *they are for all*. They demand neither money nor time. All they ask is, that we will look on them and love them with

"Pure eyes and Christian hearts."

You know, my friends, Mr. Chiswick resumed,— after one of those pauses which were made in our readings, not only for the refreshment of the reader himself, but that the other members of our small society might converse upon the subject of his lecture —you know that I have a brother, who is a huntsman; and, as I hear from those who have seen him in the field, and as I read in the *Field* itself, a very good huntsman too. Well, we had the other day a grand debate, which of us had the most difficult place to fill. "To deserve the name of a huntsman," says brother Will, "you must have a brave heart in a strong body, and a clear head in your velvet cap. You must know the natural history, character, habits, and capabilities of the three most intelligent animals in all creation (not excepting a large number of human beings, such as drunkards, gamblers, and vulpicides), the horse, the hound, and the fox. You must know every wood, plantation, spinney, and gorse covert, every field and fence, every 'earth' and drain in the hunt. You must be such an accomplished horseman, you must have such nerve, and hands, and seat, that you can either make your horse do his best at full gallop over a big un or a brook, or can make him creep step by step down, through, or up that 'very nasty place indeed,' in which there is only just room for him and for you. All the while you must be able to think on horseback, to observe the line of your fox, to watch the working of your hounds, and to restrain your 'field'; to be calm when your fox, just breaking into the sweetest country you have—all grass, and the next covert five good miles away—is headed back by a young lunatic, racing outside for a start, and makes for the woodland clays; to be serene when some fiend, in the form of a sheep-dog, chases him, and the scent is lost; to keep your temper when that chiropodist, on the rushing chestnut screw, rolls over the best hound in your pack."

"To be a good gardener," I made response, "a man must be well acquainted with geology, entomology, and meteorology" (expecting that these long scientific words would make a strong impression upon William's mind, I must confess to some disappointment upon hearing a low whistle)—" with botany, chemistry, geometry, drawing, and colour. He should have Solomon's knowledge of all trees, from the cedar to the hyssop. He should know not only from what countries his trees, shrubs, flowers, fruits, and vegetables—all things under his care, whether pleasant to the eye or good for food—are brought, but the climate, soil, and situation in which they naturally thrive. He must have both a refined taste and a persevering industry, both mental and manual skill. He should be as strong in health as the hardy Norseman, for that is a perilous life which takes men in the wintertide from the 75° of the stove to the 20° of the outer air. And with all these qualifications he must submit sometimes to be regarded as a mere hewer of wood (of tallies and pea-sticks) and drawer of water, for his plants. He must be conscious that he is occasionally considered by his fellow-creatures (alas! it may be by those whom he serves) only as a useful attendant on the cook. He must be prepared, again, to hold himself responsible for all the inclemencies of the weather, and the injuries done thereby. Like the great patriarch, he must bear the loss, whether drought or frost consume. He must listen at times to strong hints and suspicions that he has laid, incubated, and hatched all the red spiders, mealy bugs, thrip, scale, beetles, aphis, slugs, snails, grubs, and caterpillars, which gnaw the gardener's heart."

Our single-wicket match ended in "a draw." We came to no agreement on the main question. On one point, nevertheless, we were quite unanimous—namely, that a large number of individuals set up to be huntsmen and gardeners because they possess one or two of the many qualifications required. "I know a fellow" said Will, "who considers himself quite A1 as a huntsman, because he has won two or three steeple-chases, and can ride eight stone 'with notice.' When there are spectators, he is looking for a big fence, instead of looking at his hounds, and his main object in life appears to be to 'pound the field.' Half the determination to kill his fox which he exhibits in his efforts to kill himself, would make him a great reputation. Another thinks himself qualified to carry a horn because his father and his uncle hunted hounds; and a third feels himself quite equal to take command of 'the Quorn,' because he has been for four seasons one of the most incompetent whips in England.* There are plenty of them who can do one thing well; who can do well, or at all events look well, in the saddle—who can buy horses, corn, and meal, breed hounds and bring them out in first-rate condition; but a huntsman! why, I tell you, Frank, you would have to chuck fifty such chaps as these into a furnace, before you could get enough of the real metal to make one Will Goodall!"

"It is very much the same," I rejoined, "with gardeners. A youth has hardly been foreman for a year before he esteems himself competent to preside at Chatsworth. He thinks himself a grape-grower, because he has thinned a few large bunches of grapes; a plantsman, because he has produced a huge caladium or coleus; a master in arboriculture, because

* "I've a very unpleasant duty to perform this morning," said a noble and sarcastic master of hounds to his friend, as they rode to the meet. "I've an apology to make to my two whips. I told them the other day that they were the two biggest fools in England, and I've been out since with Lord ——'s hounds, and *seen two bigger!*"

there happens to be a nice Wellingtonia, planted when he was a baby, in the grounds of the place in which he lives. Nay, not a few of our older gardeners quietly ignore, or openly depreciate, important branches of their art. 'We don't go in for fruit—we are not great here in kitchen stuff—our soil is too light for this, or too heavy for that,' they say.

"Now it's all very well for a gardener to have a specialty, to try for excellence and perfection in some one department (and I would advise him to do so where his range is limited), always stipulating that nothing of consequence shall be neglected; but never, so long as I am in the flesh, and one black ball excludes, shall that man be admitted into the 'Six of Spades' who contracts and confines his admiration to some particular pursuit in horticulture, and sees no charm beyond; who, excelling in fruits, takes no notice of flowers—or succeeding in stove and greenhouse plants, will hardly look at the outdoor garden, the rosary, the fernery, the alpine or herbaceous plants. The true gardener loves them all, and wherever or whenever he finds either beauty or cultural skill, there and then his heart is glad. But I fear that there are many who declare themselves to be passionately fond of a garden who only care for a little bit of it; and I have seen those who were 'never tired of gazing on the darling flowers,' signally defeated in single combat with an honest, humbug-hating yawn. I could tell you of a pretender who came from one of the principal places in England to see another yet more beautiful than his own, and when he found that there were no orchids, he passed through the spring gardens as quickly as though he was late with a letter of importance for the post, and then spent the rest of his day in an adjoining public-house. You say, Will, that many a man blows the huntsman's horn who knows but little of his craft; and I say that many a man plays Flora's fiddle who is master of but one tune."

This conversation came into my thoughts when I began to consider what I should say to you of Summer Bedding-Out; and you will accept it, I hope, as an illustration of a fact, which all true gardeners must acknowledge and deplore—namely, that while this branch of modern horticulture absorbs with many of our brotherhood an undue proportion of their time and thought, by many others it is not justly appreciated and by some is absolutely denounced. I have spoken of the first of these extremes; let me say now, referring to the latter, that the man who can look upon beds, well arranged, of these summer beauties, bright with a soft splendour when the evening sun is low, and feel no admiration nor enjoyment, does not realize my idea of a florist. What, think you, would our gardening grandfathers say if they could return to gaze on those glowing groups of Stella and Cybister, Lady Constance Grosvenor, and fifty other scarlet, carmine, and crimson pelargoniums; the roseate blushes of Christine, Rendatler, Amaranth, Miss Rose Peach, &c. (how much do we owe to Donald Beaton in the past, and to John Pearson and others in the present, for these beautiful bedding-flowers!); the verbena's rich, kingly purple; the lobelia's brilliant blue; the dwarf ageratum's softer shade of grey; the calceolaria's golden sheen; the clear bright yellow of the pansy and marigold; the deeper hues of the gazania, tagetes, and tropæolum; the varied tints of the petunia, from white to velvety purple, pale pink to dark maroon,—how could they look on these jewels, in their setting of emerald, this exquisite picture, framed by dark glossy evergreens, or (as at beautiful Hardwicke) by tall graceful arches of honeysuckle and the climbing rose, and not confess that the scene before them, as a brilliant display of floral beauty, outshone their brightest dreams?

"Will you be good enough," I hear it said, in satirical tones, by some resolute opponent of the summer system, "to invite your gardening grandfathers to stay the night; and will you oblige me by supposing that, while their ghostships are in bed, one of those little incidents, not uncommon in this country, which go by the name of thunderstorms, shall 'drench our steeples, drown our cocks,' and play upon your bedding-out? And will you favour me with your opinion as to what those ancient florists would say, when they looked out o' window next morning, and saw how your fine-weather sailors had weathered the storm—how, with heads drooping, and all the colour gone from their faces, they crouched, limp and draggled, naked and crippled, wrecked and broken-hearted, gazing in mute despair upon all their torn and faded finery, floating upon the green sea around?"

I must honestly answer, that if the beauty of summer bedding-out depended upon the flowers to which I have referred, these ghostly gardeners would say that they preferred a thousandfold the simpler

THE SIX OF SPADES.

prettiness, which no rains could mar, of their hardy and varied plants, and shrubs, and trees, to the brilliant but ephemeral splendour which delighted them yestereve. I should feel, speaking as a cricketer, that the satirical opponent had made a clean hit for six, and that there must be a change of bowling. Messrs. Flower and Bloom being too much alike in style, I should substitute for one of them Mr. Leaf. The alternation is irresistible.

Since my first acquaintance with the bedding-out system, and I have known it almost from its birth, I have always advised, and introduced into my own garden, a large proportion of those plants which have beautiful foliage, simply because, being weather-proof, they are attractive from first to last, from the time of their appearance in the beds to their removal for safety, or destruction by frost. When koniga, and cerastium, and Flower of the Day, and Manglesii, and Golden Chain (still one of the best) geraniums (we knew not then in our terrible ignorance why they should be called pelargoniums, and I have been told that there are still two or three gardeners in very obscure localities who are not quite clear on the subject)—when these were our only foliage plants, I used them largely; and well I remember the joyous welcome which we gave to Bijou and Alma, Cloth-of-Gold and Golden Fleece (I once saw it designated as "golden fleas"), as more recently to the lovely Flower of Spring, Crystal Palace Gem, and May Queen.

Not with the same unmixed gratification do I recall the introduction of the darker foliage. I obtained seed of perilla nankinensis before any of my neighbours knew of it, and I determined to galvanize them in the succeeding summer with a shock of astonishment, and to turn them green with jealousy. I turned myself black instead. My vaulting ambition overjumped itself by several feet, and I came down in the mud before my tittering friends. You know how sparingly this melancholy leaf must be used, and you will therefore readily imagine the effect produced in a garden of which it was made the predominant feature, appearing in more than half the beds. I can only compare its aspect to that of one of the ugliest objects with which I am acquainted, and, I venture to add, most unchristian also, for it suggests neither faith nor hope—the top of a funereal hearse.

After this, as you know, our gardens were enriched by the far more cheerful and charming leaves of the iresine and amaranthus, coleus and beet. These are grand additions, and are most effective in combination with the bright summer flowers, and in contrast with other foliage plants, such as the gold and silver-leafed pelargoniums, the centaurea and polemonium (both introduced as bedders by Mr. David Thomson, then at Archerfield), the pyrethrum and variegated veronica. Some complain of difficulties in cultivation, but no plants are more easily propagated from cuttings than the coleus and iresine, or from seed than the amaranthus, beet, and perilla. I always throw in a good trowelful of rich manure when planting the iresine and amaranthus (of the former, Lindeni and Acuminata are very superior to Herbstii), harden off my coleus Verschaffeltii carefully and gradually, and plant the second week in June. In adverse weather, coleus, amaranthus, and iresine may look unhappy, and even lose some leaves at first; but if their feet are kept warm in the socks which I have recommended, they will soon recover. Beet and perilla require no coddling.

Who forgets his first interview with Mrs. Pollock—how he gazed in fascination upon those lovely tricolor leaves, then worth half-a-crown apiece? The story was told of an enthusiastic florist, that he noticed one morning a sudden and mysterious alteration in the demeanour of his wife. She was cold, sullen, and morose. Insisting upon an explanation, he was reluctantly and tearfully told that he had been murmuring in his sleep fond praises of "a Mrs. Pollock"! Mrs. P., Lady Cullum, and Sophie Dumaresque are the best in this section for planting *en masse*.

And then the bronzes—very striking and effective when properly grown and grouped, and, so far from being injured by our summer storms, smiling upon us more brightly than ever, when they have been "washed, just washed in a shower." I have been very successful with Luna, Mrs. Longfield, and Beauty of Calderdale—but I now prefer, with much gratitude to the raisers, Messrs. Downie, Laird, & Laing, Crown Prince, Imperatrice Eugenie, Lord Rosslyn, and Marquis of Lorne. The variegated ivies, too, are extremely pretty, whether as beds or as edgings. Mr. Grieve, of Culford, showed to me, at the Provincial Exhibition of the Royal Horticultural Society at Birmingham, a new variety, having a black and gold horse-shoe on a bright green ground, very distinct, and sure to be popular.

I did not mention, when speaking of the darker foliage, the oxalis and the alternanthera, because the former seems too earth-like in colour to be effective in beds; and the latter has been, with me, capricious and weakly. I also think that echeverias and sempervivums are more appropriate to the rockery than to the summer garden; and I am inclined to believe that a snug nook in the same habitation will prove most suitable for that exquisite gem, Mesembryanthemum cordifolium variegatum, with its bright little purple flowers peeping out from its golden leaves.

And these latter words remind me how many of our plants with variegated foliage have beautiful flowers as well—to wit, of pelargoniums, Flower of Spring, May Queen, Silver Nosegay, Bijou, Cloth-of-Gold, Crystal Palace Gem, Golden Fleece, the tricolors, and bronzes, and ivies.

Let me therefore advise that in the summer garden foliage and flowering plants be intermixed, in circles, diamonds, panels, à la pincushion, and in other designs, so that the one may support the other, both in prosperity and in adversity, both in wet weather and in dry.

When I have added to this, dig well, dung well, put out plants few and good, rather than numerous and scraggy, but such as will eventually quite cover your beds, note down the defects of this year's arrangement, that you may correct them hereafter, keep your ears open when visitors come, and your eyes when you go a-visiting,—I have only to thank you for your kind patience, and to resume my pipe.

CHAPTER X.

MR. EVANS ON SHOWS AND SHOWING.*

Mr. CHAIRMAN and gents all, this is the only meeting of the Six of Spades which I don't go to quite so cheerfully as a wasp to a ripe apricot. You see, I'm hardly much more of a scholar than the chap as only went to school one Tuesday, and master was absent a-measuring land; and when I've got to speak to them as has had good eddication, I feel about as comfortable as a tomtit a-cherupping to a lot of nightingales. Howsomever, I must take my part, and if you'll excuse mistakes and plain speaking, I think you'll find me there or thereabouts in facts; for I've been concerned with flower-shows best part of my time, and after all, as I've heard my father say, an ounce of experience will win more prizes than two stone and a half of grammar.

Consequently, and by your leave, Mr. Chairman and gents all, I will make a few observations, first, on the best way of getting up and managing a flower-show; and, secondly, on showing plants, and flowers, and cetrers.

Fine folks, as comes a-yawning and a-drawling, and a-sniffing and a-sneering, into a flower-show, and as ups with an eyeglass to look at a plant, just under

---

* I have transcribed Mr. Evans's MS. *verbatim*, but only *literatim* when his peculiar views in etymology, chiefly of a phonetic character, seemed more specially to illustrate the manner and the man.

their noses, as if it was half a mile off, and then, having picked out the poorest specimen in all the place, pronounces the whole affair a failure,—they little thinks what time, and trouble, and what money too, has been spent to produce what they see, or rather I should say, what they won't see, before them. Just let me try to describe what has to be done aforehand. First of all, some five or six sperrity young gardeners, led on by a brace of rich amateurs, as full o' beans and as keen to show their paces as a pair of London Park 'osses—they meets and passes a resolution, that nothing but a flower-show on an extensive scale can save the county from disgrace. They forms a committee, and they calls a general meeting. A few more lively florists turn up, together with a timber merchant, who proposes himself to the company as stage-manager; three publicans, glowing with desire to refresh the weary and athirst; a merry individual who has to do with tents, and who "hopes that having canvassed their votes, they will kindly vote for his canvas;" and a party who has got the best field in all England for a flower-show, and is agreeable to let it for two days on payment of half of its yearly rent. Then the editor of the local newspaper, who has just discovered all of a sudden what a tremendous interest he takes in horticulture, and who has offered to do all the printing at a mere nominal profit (of something like 300 per cent.), he writes a beautiful piece in the *Dull-borough Eagle* about this influential, energetic, and successful meeting, and invites the earnest attention of his readers to an advertisement, which will be found in another part of its columns. Well, all goes on as smooth and easy as a new mowing-machine, until the committee begins to collect subscriptions, and then there's pebbles among the knives. I've been round myself, and though it's very delightful to hear what a vast amount of charity there is in the world, as nobody knows nothing of, and what a many calls folks has, and how still they answers 'em, it ain't pleasant to arrive, as somehow one generally does, just after the last entry has been made on the subscription list, and there's nothing for you but best wishes. I once went a-begging for a cottager's show to Sir Nathan Nipper, knight and drysalter, him as they sent for when the great engineer swallowed the half-sovereign—"for if it's gold," they said, "Nat'll have it;" and he says to me, "Mr. Bevins" (the old screw knew my name well enough), "I can assure you that it positively makes me tremble to think of the amount which I have given away during the last twelve months in charity." Whereupon my mate, as formed along with me what our committee called a deppytation, a young clergyman, and one of the pluckiest gentlemen as ever I had the pleasure of meeting, he turns as red as a Tom Thumb geranium, and out it comes—"Sir Nathan," he says, "everybody knows that you have more than a million of money, and your head-gardener told us this morning that you had just spent two hundred pounds in orchids; and yet you cannot spare a sovereign in support of a poor man's show. The best wish I can wish you is, that you may really tremble as you pretend to do at your miserable list of charities.

You need not ring the bell; we're going." And oh, how pleased I felt when we were fairly out of his park!

Some refuses point-blank. "We do not desire," they says, very cutting and haughty, "to have our gardens covered with fat cucumbers, from two feet to three feet long; or to see one bunch of grapes, which we may not eat, upon a vine, instead of six which we may. These flower-shows demoralize the people. They make them idle, and discontented, and luxurious."

But there's kind folks to be found for searching, and so at last perseverance wins, and there's a sufficient fund, given or promised, to start the undertaking. Then comes the grand meeting of subscribers, "to arrange preliminaries, and to draw up a schedule." And sometimes this general meeting is not unlike a general engagement. Four more happy owners of the finest site in Europe for a show appear upon the scene, several more licensed victuallers very anxious to cheer their fellow-creatures with the best of beer and spirits, rival contractors, opposition printers, and a new purveyor of tents. Then comes the question of music. Some says Coldstreams, some says Grenadiers, and some says native talent. Farmer Horsman is for the Yeomanry, and Ensign Foote is for the Volunteers, and Captain Port wishes to remind the meeting that no regiment in the service has a better bandmaster than Herr Herewig, of the Militia. Next round, and it's generally a good un, is about amusements. Young Mr. Joy, having previously winked confidential at his friends, and pointed with his thumb in the direction of old Jaundice, rises to propose that the flower-show shall be connected with a general gala, including a great variety of entertainments, and terminating in a brilliant display of fireworks. Old J. rushes at the bait, like a 10-lb. pike at a gudgeon. If, says he, this opportunity of refining the public mind by the exhibition of things beautiful, and by the encouragement of an innocent recreation, is to be turned into an occasion of stuffing, and swilling, and smoking, and niggers, and pig balloons, and Punch and Judys, he must beg to remove his name from the committee.

Then comes the schedule of prizes. Mr. Tank suggests that stove plants should always take precedence, and that it is very desirable to restrict competition to exhibitors residing in the county. Mr. Heath remarks that any old woman with a big boiler, and an old tooth-brush to rub off the scale, can grow them crotons, and suchlike, and that the chief evidence of real talent is to be found in the successful cultivation of New Holland plants. Mr. Bunch, whose employer some three years ago erected a long range of vineries and peacheries, has always noticed that the British public take a wonderful delight in fruit. Mr. Moss observes that ferns make a show by themselves. Mr. Kindly maintains that the chief object of the society should be, to extend the love of the beautiful among the poor, and recommends prizes of an insane amount for bunches of wild flowers. Mr. Brierly would like to be informed whether the rose-tent isn't always the most crowded of all, and proposes three silver cups for the queen of flowers. Mr.

Tooth thinks that, when all's said and done, a good mealy potato takes a deal o' beating, and so does peas and ham. You see, Mr. Chairman and gents all, the old saying is a true one, that—

> " Different people has different opinions—
> Some likes horchids, and some likes hinions."

But the question now is, not what this man or that man fancies the most, but what is best to be done in establishing a flower-show; and on this point I have, if you please, a few words of advice to give.

We must bear in mind, in the first place, that not many folks are as fond of flowers as we are; that most people have no inclination, and, if they had, no time nor means to grow them to perfection; that they may love flowers, and not care for flower-shows; that we are only riding our own hobby, and that neighbours prefer their own hacks. And so we mustn't be impatient in asking help, and must give to subscribers not only our thanks, but certain advantages with regard to tickets and early admission to the show.

The committee should be formed of the best gardeners, and the best men of business, who will promise to attend, with a zealous amateur as honorary secretary and treasurer, and a good accountant, well paid, to do the work.

A nobleman, or gentleman of high position, should be solicited annually to act as president, beginning with some one who will fill his house for the show, and set the example of giving a £5 cup. The public is still very fond o' dukes; but if a peer cannot be engaged, the best must be made of some young M.P. as durstn't say No for his life.

As to choice of ground, it's best to get near a railway station, to have a good approach, and a good entrance, and plenty of room for your tents, bands, and cetrer. I say tents, because it's a mistake to have a flower-show under slates instead of under canvas. If there isn't a crowd, it won't pay; and if there is a crowd, there's no getting out of it. There's certain fishes as don't want to meet other fishes, and there should be plenty of sea-room for all. The best o' friends don't like being jammed together, like a load o' linseed-cake; and if you gets a Whig boot on a Tory corn, or a Low Church elbow into Broad Church ribs, you'll interfere with harmony. I see a pair of ladies once, as weren't on speaking terms, squeezed together in the middle of a crowd, until they looked like a two-headed nightingale. Then a band in a room! you might just as well bring our Church organ and play it in this garden-house. And, I'll just add here, being on music, if you've a decent band near home, stick to neighbours, and they'll stick to you.

The next toepick on the tappy is the schedule or prize-list, and upon this, in my opinion, depends to a very great extent the success of the whole concern. Some committees seem to think that if they give plenty of small prizes, and so let everybody have a chance, as they say, they are sure to have a good display; but the consequence is that first-rate gardeners won't sacrifice their time or risk their plants for such paltry rewards; the public is disgusted with a collection of rubbish, and a lot of fourth-rate exhibitors go home and tell their friends that they have been and whopped the world, because their betters wouldn't take the trouble to cool their self-conceit. I say the public is disgusted, as well they may be, because when folks goes out a-visiting, they don't expect to be set down to gingerbread nuts and cockles; whereas, if you gives them a first-class round o' beef, there's few or none complains. And on this principle I always say, give a few fat prizes rather than a many lean ones. If you offer a prize of £10 for twelve stove and greenhouse plants, half of them to be in bloom; a £5 prize for a collection of fruit; and give a good prize for vegetables, you will have something worth seeing in the different departments of horticulture—something for your visitors to admire, and for your gardeners to copy. "But £10 for a dozen plants," I once heard a rich citizen say; "why, you'd buy the lot for £5." I kept silence, but I thought that I should like to see the countenance of Mr. Thomas Baines, or of Mr. Benjamin Williams, on receiving the offer; and I doubted whether the politeness of Mr. William Cole would stand such a provocation.

Start well, my advice is, if you starts at all; but don't go sowing cinders and expecting kidney-beans. They wins who ventures most. Did you ever hear what Mr. Bruce Findlay, the curator of the Manchester Botanical Gardens, recommended the council to do, when their shows was failures, and their funds was low? Why, to give a thousand pounds in prizes, and to have the best national exhibition which the best gardeners in England could produce during the Whitsun holiday week. It was enough to set this council's teeth a-chattering; but Lancashire lads ta'es a deal o' scaring, and they makes answer, "We'll find the brass." Well, that show was a grand success, and has been every year since; the receipts last May, if I am not mistaken, being over £1600. And most of this in shillings, from hard-working men and women! How bright the flowers must seem to those poor factory hands, who've been stooping over warp and woof! How sweet the roses must smell, after all that oil and grease! How merry must the music sound, after all that clank and whir! Brother Spades, I can't think of 'em without thanking God that He has sent me to work in the fresh pure air among the flowers and fruits; and may His blessing be, as it surely will, on all those kindly men as make parks, and playgrounds, and plan holiday trips, for them as toils in the mill!

Now a few words about arranging plants and flowers for a show. There should be, wherever there can be, and there might be at most public gardens, a place laid out for the purpose, with raised mounds and sloping banks surrounding, and broad gravel walks within, as at the Manchester shows, of which I have been speaking, at the shows of the Royal Botanic Society in the Regent's Park, and of the Royal Horticultural Society in the provinces. This ground may be made ornamental at all times, and is soon covered with canvas when it is wanted for a show. Where such advantages cannot be had, the most effective, quickest, and cheapest plan is to group the larger plants on the ground, having a good supply of spare pots and blocks for raising and tilting when necessary, and to protect them with cords and stakes. Of course you must have stages, where you have no banks, for small plants, cut flowers, fruit, and vegetables; but the less timber you display the better. Three or four members of the committee, as have taste in arranging, should be told off on the morning of the show to superintend "the staging."

As concerns amusements, it's no good a-howling and a-scriking because flower-shows by themselves, with some few exceptions, won't pay expenses, or because nine-tenths of our fellow-creatures prefers a balloon to a bougainvillea, and likes fireworks better than fuchsias. While you and I feast our eyes on the flowers, why shouldn't Jack have his grin at the clowns, and Jill her dance on the green? Folks can be merry and modest too; and I've seen 'em a-drinking and a-smoking at the sign of the "Six of Spades," and elsewhere, without getting very drunk. If the rich thinks the poor has low tastes, let 'em join a little more in their amusements, and so raise 'em higher; but I'm inclined to fancy that there's less harm done in shooting at a target for nuts than in crippling pigeons for five-pound notes; and I'm sure that there's more lying, and swearing, and robbing, and drunkenness at one of the great race meetings, with fine lords and ladies a-looking on, than at all the flower-shows and galas put together. Besides, if the people won't come to flower-shows without some other inducements, how are we to teach them a taste for flowers? He who comes for the fun is sure to walk through the tents; and many a man who left home to hear the niggers (why are they considered to be so genteel at St. James's Hall, and so "vulgar" everywhere else?) has gone back to think more of his garden.

And this brings me to speak of prizes for cottagers. Now you can't do a poor man a greater kindness, in my opinion, than by giving him a garden, and encouraging him in every way to take an interest in it; and, after many years of experience, I feel convinced that the best way to do this, so far as shows are concerned, is to have separate exhibitions for cottagers in the village schoolrooms, and not to tack 'em on to those larger meetings at which they cannot possibly receive the attention and the notice which they well deserve. White and black currants don't get much praise where there's Muscat and Hamburg grapes; and nobody cares, after looking at dipladenias and allamandas and ixoras, for the poor little window-plant. That posy of Mary Smith's in the blue and white mug, with its bits of totter-grass and ferns, is as pretty in my eyes as anything in all the show; but nine out of ten whom I ask to admire it invite me, with a smile o' pity, to go and look at Lady Bigge's bouquet of orchids. Some says, let the cottagers have a tent to themselves, and they sticks 'em in a corner, like a peep-show at a fair behind Wombwell's menagerie; but I says, let 'em have a show and a holiday to themselves, and let all their neighbours go and help 'em, not only with their money, but with kind words, which is better than silver, and brotherly love, which is brighter than gold. There ain't a happier sight to be seen than the people of one place, high and low, gathered together, with goodwill to each other in their hearts. And we gardeners, mind you, have much in our power, and may do our part, with our spare seeds, and our spare plants, and that better knowledge which our practice brings.

The best time for a flower-show in the country is between the hay and corn harvests, about the beginning of July. It's a little late for plants, and a little early for fruit, but good prizes will bring both in abundance. And it's the best time for roses. If this date is inconvenient, the second week in September, when the harvest is generally over, and the squires are home among the partridges, is a favourable time ; and you'll have foliage plants, ferns, gladioli, hollyhocks, dahlias, asters, and any amount of fruit.

I've only one more hint to give about shows, before I speak about showing. Let it be well and widely known that tickets which will be charged one shilling on the day of the exhibition, may be purchased at various places for sixpence any day before it. When a treasurer has heard the night before the show that several thousands have been sold, his behaviour next morning under rain is beautiful.

Is it a good thing for gardeners to show ? That's a question as should have a cautious answer, about as cautious as a speech which I once heard from a shrewd old Spade to a bumptious young un, who asked him how he grew his prize calceolarias ? The question seemed to me a goodish bit cooler than cucumbers, because he who put it had showed against

him to whom it was put on several occasions in this
very class; and it sounded very like a request made
by a soldier in battle to his enemy for the loan of his
sword, with a view to digging it into the owner's ribs.
I cocked both ears, I can tell you, to catch what the
old man would say; and, after looking a bit confused,
and scratching his brain for a brace o' seconds, slowly
and solemnly he said this: "In growing the herbaceous calceolaria for exhibition in pots, we find from
experience that everything depends upon everything
else, and we act according*ly*."

So to the question, "Is it a good thing that
gardeners should exhibit?" we answers cautious, "It
depends." If the master is willing, and the gardener
has time and talent (he'll find the time if he has got
the talent, by beginning work sooner or ending it
later), let him show by all means. The hope of
success will be to him one of them happy thoughts
which lighten his daily toil, as the thought of a
holiday to a lad at his sums, of a Fair day to a farm-
boy at his plough, or of a Review day to a volunteer
at drill. Besides the Great Light of all, we needs
these bits of brightness on our journey, and the same
kind mercy sends them. Then the show itself will
cheer him up if he wins, and teach him if he loses;
and, win or lose, it is good for us gardeners to see
plants, flowers, fruit, and vegetables as perfect as
care and skill can make them, and to find out, as far
as possible, how this has been done. If I were the
proprietor of a large garden, I should like my
gardener to go to exhibitions, whether he exhibited or
not; and I know several wealthy and wise masters

who every now and then send their head-gardeners to London to visit the nurseries and the shows.

Of course there's a risk that gardeners who show may shirk some of their duties, in order that they may give more time to favourites. But it will be found that, as a rule, though there are many exceptions, they who show successful will have other things, besides those in which they takes a lead, a little better in quality and more abundant in quantity than their neighbours, because they have more chances of seeing that which is the best in its class, and of learning how to humour it.

So we will suppose, if you please, that it has been decided by master and gardener that the latter is to show, and pass on to the next question which comes afore us, and that is, What to show? It's a big question, because a great many exhibitors fails from trying to do too much. I remember reading in the newspapers that, when a few of our cavalry went a-galloping at Balaklava into the middle of the Russian army, one of them French generals remarked that it was grand, but it wasn't war; and it's no good for a gardener, however much he may know, to go a-charging on his bit of a spanned-roofed greenhouse against a man with half a mile of glass. He may now and then win a victory over some one bigger but slower than himself, just as you've seen a game bantam cock make a great Cochin stride off in search of his mother; but whenever he meets a gardener who knows as much as he does, with more room and resources, why, weight and size must tell, and the lesser bird will get the spur in the brain. No doubt we should all of us like to show Lælia purpurata with sixty-four spikes of bloom as some of us have seen it shown, tree-ferns almost too tall to travel under the railway arch, Thrinax elegans eight feet by six feet, anæctochilus in brewing-tubs, and azaleas in soft-water butts; no doubt we all have the talent to do so; but. if we have not the space nor the means, perhaps we had better select something which we can grow, and, what's more, grow to perfection.

In my younger days one of my masters came to me and said,—"Evans, I am going to enlarge the stove and the little New Holland house, and we'll go in for specimen plants." Well, the addition of a few new lights made our tiny places look quite grand in our eyes. I was sent to London to purchase plants, and returned from the nurseries of Messrs. Veitch, Williams, Bull, Lee, Henderson, and Fraser, with the nicest lot of young stuff for training you ever set your eyes on. So with the best of turf, peat, sphagnum, and sand, and with any amount of heat and moisture in my stove, and of light and air for my hardier plants, I went to work in earnest. Of course I had to fight the usual foes. Fungus sprung up in my bed of tan, until one gardener as came a-visiting very nearly got his head punched for inquiring, as he entered the stove, whether it was our house for mushrooms; mealy-bug and scale did not forget us; but time and resolution, turpentine and patience, overcame them all, and my plants started off a-growing like custard-marrows in a hotbed. It was very pleasant to watch them for the first two seasons, and master was in and out continual, talking about this show and that show, and the cups we were going to win; but when, in the third spring, they began a-rawming and a-scrawming * all over the house, and to rub themselves against the roof, looking something like a swan in a hen-coop, and seeming to say, "How could you bring us into such a poky place as this?" when the Thief-Palm unfolded a leaf about the size of a small door, and Alocasia macrorhiza favoured us with foliage having the circumference of a large tea-tray,—we began to find out that we had made a mistake, and to feel as uncomfortable about our numerous and growing family as the old woman who lived in a shoe. And the worst of it was, that after all our trouble, when we had selected our twelve for exhibition (three of them, I remember, were taken out through the roof, the door being much too narrow) we were signally defeated by a nurseryman from a distance, who had plants to which ours were pigmies.

Let no gardener, who has only a moderate space under glass, attempt to show collections of stove and greenhouse plants, but let him either confine himself to some special class, such as the Gloxinia for the stove and the Pelargonium for the greenhouse, or, using his houses for general purposes, let him exhibit in some other department—hardy flowers, or vegetables, or fruit. Let him consider what he *can* do, and then determine to do it thoroughly. Let him never rest

---

* "Rawm" I believed to be a corruption of roam, and I was powerless to throw any light upon "scrawm," when a floral friend explained that the two words had been corrupted from *rambling* and *scrambling*, by pronouncing broadly the first vowel, and eliminating a consonant and liquid altogether.

satisfied until "First Prize" is nailed on his box. There's only one exhibition in which I should prefer to be second, and that's an exhibition of genteel brutality which they calls a duel. Let him make up his mind, I say, to excel in something, and there's as much honour and as much happiness to be found in producing twelve first-rate Auriculas as in the display of twelve haycocks o' bloom as have filled two trucks on the rail.

And now I must warn exhibitors, that although we gardeners are as honest as other folks (we ought to be a little bit more so, and I sometimes venture to think that we are, because we work so near to God), they will meet now and then with certain dodges and deceptions invented to mislead them by a few flora-sharpers, who, if they can't win by honours, will try to win by tricks. Three times, my brothers, have I been done by them individuals several shades browner than pleased my taste.

On the first occasion, it is true, I was taken in quite good-humouredly, only for the fun of the thing, and could not have won under any circumstances, but somehow I didn't like it. My master had backed me against the gardener of a relation, who lived in the neighbourhood, to exhibit twelve pansies in pots at the next local flower-show; and I was rather surprised to hear, only a week before the exhibition, that we were invited to pay a visit in the family way (I was often taken out for a holiday of this kind by my employer—a true brother gardener) and go into the enemy's camp. We went accordingly, and in walking round the gardens we came upon an uncovered frame, in which were twelve pansies in pots. No remark was made on them, and we just passed leisurely by, as though nobody thought much interest about them; but we made the most of time and eyesight. And the consequence was, that we were in tip-top spirits during the rest of our visit; and when we were out of the grounds, and master asked me what I thought of his wager, I remember that I answered, "It's a Ribston Pippin to a Siberian Crab on our lot, unless the gents as is going to judge prefers fourpenny-bits to florins!" Well, the show-day came, and the judges came, and they preferred, both to fourpennies and florins, some crown-pieces which came, in the form of twelve plants much finer than ours, and were shown by—our relation! Their prize specimens were concealed in the asparagus bed all the time of our visit; and when the race came, they sailed away from us, like a yot from a barge full o' coals.

Disappointment number two comed some time afterwards, when, having a good deal of glass under my charge, I used to grow some large specimen plants. On one occasion I had some twenty of these in readiness for a grand floral exhibition, which was to be held same time with our county agricultural show, and I was naturally very anxious to win a special prize of twenty pounds that was offered for twelve stove and greenhouse plants. Looking round, on the morning of the exhibition, I saw that I had only one man to fear, a stranger who had brought from a distance some plants quite as good as my own, with others of an inferior quality. I must tell

you that there was another special prize of five
pounds for six stove and greenhouse, and a third of
two pounds for a single specimen, and that we both
of us showed in the three classes. Well, as soon as
we had "staged," I went to have a squint at the
enemy, and I was rejoiced to find that though he
knew as much as I did about growing, he seemed to
know precious little about showing, plants. He put
up a very good single specimen, but not the best he
had; he showed four first-rate plants in his six, with
two altogether inferior; and in his twelve there were
some seven grand specimens, with three common-
place, and two bad enough to condemn the lot. In
consequence of this, I made some changes, setting
my best plant against his single specimen, and
distributing my others so as to secure the first prize
throughout. I was to win in all. There could be no
doubt about it, and all my brother gardeners said so.

I remembered afterwards that just as we were
leaving the big tent for the judges to come in, my
opponent sent back his assistant to find a syringe
which he had left among the plants. Perhaps you
guess what that gentleman, not finding the squirt,
amused himself in doing? At all events, when we
exhibitors were readmitted into the show, I found
that he had transferred his single specimen (substi-
tuting a rubbishy old Caladium, worth about three
shillings, and having the oudacious impudence to
place it side by side with my best Ixora), together
with the best four out of his six, to his twelve, of
course removing the invalids, and so (succeeding
in his little game, which was to make me divide

my forces) had won the £20 prize, and only left me £7.

You'd think an old fish that had twice been pricked would be very hard to catch; but once again, and that no long time since, I took the bait that was dangled before me, and gulped it down hook and all. I thought myself quite sure of a special prize which had been offered at our annual show, for six exotic Ferns, and I had put up half a dozen very decent specimens, when another distinguished foreigner placed four as good as mine beside them, and then carelessly inquired from his foreman what other two he had brought? "There's the big Farleyense," he replied, "and that Leptopteris, which you thought of showing as a single specimen, but they're at the far end of the van, and it'll be half an hour before I can bring them." "The big Farleyense!" why, there was not at that time, as I believed, more than four or five such treasures in the country; "and the specimen Leptopteris,"—whereas I had only a pinch of Todæa under a small bell-glass. I caved in. I conveyed my Ferns into another tent, and showed for the ordinary prize given by our society. Friends, I've hardly patience to tell you that the big Farleyense was just visible to the naked eye under a great glass doom,* as would have held a pæony; and that the Leptopteris had lost its head on the journey, and came out nothing but a Pteris (argyræa) about half as good as my own.

There's another yet more dishonest deception which is practised by certain parties as cannot afford to keep

* Dome intended.

a conscience. I mean the borrowing and the showing of other people's plants. You are probably aware that the Council of the Manchester Botanical Society and the committees of several other horticultural meetings have been quite unable to see the beauty of this new form of petty larceny, and have gone at it rather free. Acting together, they certainly ought to be able to do that which one of our greatest exhibitors once did for himself—namely, to expose and to punish suspected roguery. He was informed that a certain grower of plants had promised to lend the best of them to his principal opponent at a forthcoming show; and a short time before the exhibition he paid a visit to the object of suspicion. On the day of the show the plants appeared, as he was told they would, in the collection of his adversary; but he won, nevertheless, the first prize. Rogues is often fools, and this one, after a few goes of gin, began a-comparing and complaining before the public. On this my friend, as I'm proud to call him, quietly fetches the chairman and several members of the committee, and when this floral felon was catching his wind for another innings, he says very distinct, so that every one in the tent could hear him nicely, "I demand that this exhibitor may be disqualified for showing plants which are not his own. I saw them three weeks ago in Mr. ——'s collection, and suspecting conspiracy, I put a small piece of tobacco-pipe close to the tallies of that Ixora, that Bougainvillea, that Allamanda, and that Erica. Let the secretary examine the pots." He did so, and produced the pipes. The culprit, admitting his guilt in the usual way—that is, by challenging everybody to fight—was disqualified, and struck off the list of subscribers.

I've kept you too long, and I'll only trouble you with one more bit of advice. Whatever else you show, don't show temper. If you win, don't gawster,* and if you lose, don't sulk. Always bear in mind that in Showing, as in everything else, Pluck, Patience, and Perspiration must win the day.

CHAPTER XI.

MR. GRUNDY'S SONG.

INTRODUCING to readers horticultural a song which has no connection with horticulture, I can only plead that it has been oft applauded by members of our floral brotherhood, and that I am anxious to preserve, among "things which the world would not willingly let die," a peculiar order of vocal music, long prevalent in our rural districts, but now almost superseded by the melodies of Mr. Christy and other composers. The ballads to which I refer were chanted, in the time of my boyhood, at harvest suppers and other festal meetings of our farm-labourers, and were of a tragic character. They were recited and received with great solemnity, however supernatural the incidents, however homely the diction might be. The articulation was slow, the eyes of the vocalist were fixed upon

* *Gawster*, to brag, to boast.

THE SIX OF SPADES.

the ceiling, and the sealing-waxed end of a clay-pipe rested lightly on his chin, save when at the words, "Chorus, gentlemen," it was removed a while, to serve as a conductor's baton.

In this style and spirit dear old Joe Grundy sang —sang as if he were in the Albert Hall instead of in a tiny chamber; and though the performance was a trial to some of us, who did not quite believe, as he did, every word of his startling story, and had grievous wrestlings in consequence, with terrible temptations to laugh, it nevertheless never failed to elicit the liveliest approbation from us all.

The tune is old and familiar; but, as I know not the name, I herewith transcribe the notes of it :—

MR. GRUNDY'S SONG—"SAIREY JANE JONES."

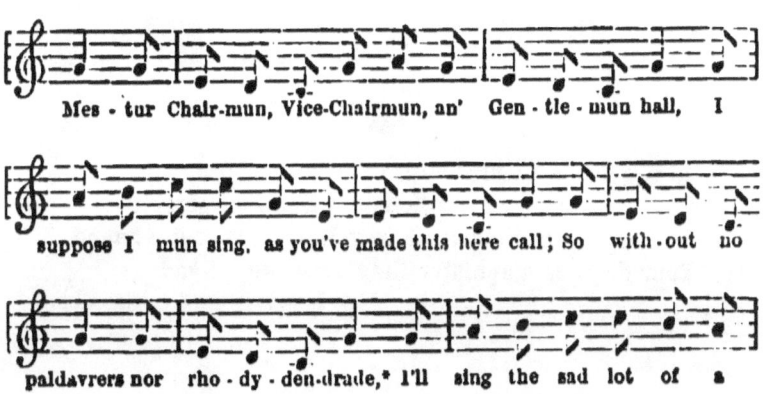

* I asked Mr. Grundy the meaning of these words, and his reply was, that he "reckoned they were poetry, and was put in for garnish." The author, I need hardly state, had palaver and rodomontade in his mind.

bew-ti-ful maid.   Ho,   clea-vers and bones! ho, Sair-ey Jane Jones! Luv ho's a rum un, as all on us howns,

II.

Sammel Cox was a butcher, young, gay, and genteel,
With an ansum blew coat, a white hapun, and steel :
He'd a sweet little cart, and no os cud trot quicker ;
But, truth for to tell, Sam was parshul to licker.
     Ho, cleavers and bones, &c.

III.

Now these here is the fax 'ow Sam Cox cum to grief :
'E went hup to the 'all with some muttin and beef,—
And there 'e first saw, with 'er smile so bewitchin',
Miss Sairey Jane Jones, the new cook in the kitchin.
     Ho, cleavers and bones, &c.

IV.

'Is 'art was a-blazin' with luv's burnin' fire,
And with tender hemotions did Sammel perspire ;
And says 'e to 'imself, Sairey Jane, my young friend,
Your days as a spinster they draws to a hend.
     Ho, cleavers and bones, &c.

V.

For days, and for weeks, and for months 'e did try
To win that fair cook with 'is tongue and 'is hi—
And at last she did promise next Sunday she'd take
A walk with Sam Cox in the wood by the lake.
     Ho, cleavers and bones, &c.

VI.

He shaved his sen close, and he soaped his sen clean,
Just like some gret Dook, when he goes to the Queen;
With some nice mutton fat then he polished 'is 'ed,
And Sairey Jane Jones you are mine, ma'am, he said.
      Ho, cleavers and bones, &c.

VII.

They walked on its banks, and they talked 'mong its trees,
Till the stars they lit hup like so many fu-zees;
But when Sammel says, Sairey luv, will you be mine?
No, says she, Butcher Cox, hi must hask to decline.
      Ho, cleavers and bones, &c.

VIII.

Hi'm fond on yer, Cox, but did long since hengage
My 'art to a butler, I'd know'd from a page.
Next month we shall wed—ah! them words 'ow they bust
  'im,
And that butler, oh mi,—'ow 'e innudly cust 'im!
      Ho, cleavers and bones, &c.

IX.

But he swallered 'is roth, and presarved 'is demeener,
And 'e looked like a lamb, though 'e felt a ihener—
And says 'e, Then next Sunday night I will bring 'ere
A nicst wedding present—a luv sowveneer.
      Ho, cleavers and bones, &c.

X.

'E went 'ome wite with ate, and to comfit 'is 'art
'E drank of neat gin somethink under a q'art;
And that night did resolve that next Sunday e'd make
A hend of Miss Jones in the wood by the lake.
      Ho, cleavers and bones, &c.

XI.

They met, and the present 'e brought for poor Jane
Was a knife, which 'e put to 'er jugyleer vein ;
And then with a fury, hi ne'er 'erd the loikes,
'E throwed fair Miss Jones to the chubs and the poikes.
                Ho, cleavers and bones, &c.

XII.

'E sailed off next morning to Ha-meri-ka,
But a storm met the ship ere she'd got arf 'er way ;—
The waves they did foam, and the lightnings did fly,
And a thunderbolt 'it Sammel Cox in the hi !
                Ho, cleavers and bones, &c.

XIII.

S. Cox hupon this lost 'is presence o' mind,
And likewise 'is legs, for a nowlin gret wind
Blow'd 'im bang overboard, and the sailors hagree
As a shark nipped 'im hup, when 'e got to the sea.
                Ho, scrunching 'is bones, havenging Miss Jones, &c.

XIV.

MORAL.

Young ladies hengaged with gay butchers don't dally,
Or p'r'aps you may meet this sad fate of Miss Sally ;
And gentilmen hall from the gin-bottle fly,
Hor a thunderbolt's sure to 'it you in the hi.
                Ho, cleavers and bones, &c.

CHAPTER XII.

MY MINIATURE GARDEN.

BY THE CURATE.

It is within the range of your sad experience that we gardeners are subject to bitter disappointments, failures, and reverses; we are not oblivious of the mealy-bug, red-spider, wire-worm, cockroach, earwig, beetle, caterpillar, snail, and slug; we are familiar with mildew, canker, and blight; we know that the mellow ouzel, fluting in the elm, has wet his whistle, and proposes to wet it again, with our cherries and other fruit; we have suffered all the ills which horticulture is heir to, from a thunderstorm to a nibbling mouse; but I maintain that a garden, well cared for, has such an infinite variety of charms, that these minute solicitudes (bah! grunts the cynic—he calls a thunderstorm a minute solicitude) only enhance its joys; and that there is no month in the year, no day in the week, in which (always supposing the existence of "a bit o' glass") there is not something new, something beautiful, to interest and to please.

Take, for example, this November month in which, so Frenchmen say, we rush in crowds to our trees for suspension, and to our streams for submersion, with a wild disdain of life; and then let me tell you, my brothers of the spade, what pleasure, and what profit also, I have had this day from my garden.

Coming this morning from our matin service, leaving our altar bright and fragrant, as, thanks to you, my friends, it ever is, with the loveliest flowers which art can rear, the sweetest, purest offering, surely, that we can return to Him,

"Whose breath perfumes them, and whose pencil paints,"—

I cut a bouquet of the last roses of autumn (Dijon's Glory, generous Jules Margottin, brave Maréchal

Vaillant, and fair Souvenir de Malmaison), intermixing a few bits of hardy ferns and of feathers from the pampas grass. After breakfast, writing a sermon with part of my posy before me (if I am here dispelling an illusion that, because I preach without a manuscript, I preach without any written preparation, so much the better), I refreshed myself twice by peeping into my little houses, by a hasty survey of my treasures, in vinery, greenhouse, and stove. For luncheon I had a luscious Beurré d'Amanlis pear, which I consolidated with a brace of dry biscuits, and medicated with a glass of sherry. In the afternoon I had a dig in my kitchen-garden, which made me feel as though I could swarm up the greasiest pole, and eat the leg of mutton afterwards; and then in my parochial walk I took two portions from the bouquet aforesaid, and two small bunches of grapes, to four of my sick folk; and I would that a certain earnest and eloquent London preacher, who told us, at our Nottingham Church Congress, that we clergy were not to entertain the desire of becoming good gardeners —I would that he had seen the smiles which welcomed both flowers and fruit.

It is written that, in the year 1583, the General Chapter at Cisteaux sent a commissioner to Scotland, to visit and reform the monks of Melrose, who, with other charges, were accused of possessing each one a pleasure-garden of his own. And the historian proceeds to say that, when summoned to a meeting at Edinburgh, these clerical gardeners defended themselves with great skill and ability. I should like to have heard them plead. I see in imagination a bright-eyed brother, producing reverently an ancient Hebrew manuscript, and asking the commissioner to note the 8th verse of the 2nd chapter of the Book of Genesis : " And the Lord God planted a garden eastward in Eden ; and there He put the man whom He had formed ; " and another comes forward with parchment pages of Greek, and he points to the word Gethsemane, and to the 41st verse of St. John's 19th chapter : " Now in the place where He was crucified there was a garden ; and in the garden a new sepulchre, wherein was never man yet laid." And then I hear them urge that a garden was to them a place of holy recollections, of humble penitence, of faithful hope, as well as of refreshment, and rest, and peace.

Grave and solemn though his vocation be, the country parson " nevertheless " (as good George Herbert writes) " sometimes refresheth himself, as knowing that nature will not bear everlasting droopings," and " because all men shun the company of perpetual severity ; " and where shall he refresh himself so healthfully, so harmlessly, as in a garden ?

Let me try to prove this yet more practically—to assert not only the happy influence, but the profitable use of horticulture, by borrowing friend Chiswick's Fairy and Gourd, and by taking you in imagination through my garden-ground. And I have a favour to ask, before we step into the pumpkin,—do not think me Pharisaic when I speak of the little gifts which go from my garden to the poor ; do not liken me to that proud young Horner who displayed his fruit, and withal his arrogance ; do not regard me as the trumpeter of my own praises, but as a true knight coming forth to do battle for our royal lady, our Flora, the Queen of Spades!

Enter first, if you please, my kitchen-garden. In front of that wall, which has a southern aspect, and in the warm border, between wall and walk, I raise annually from seed such an abundance of greens,* cabbages, cauliflowers, lettuces, &c., as supplies not only my own requirements, but many a cottage-garden besides; while in the dry sheds built behind this wall, I have a good store of onions, beet, carrots, turnips, &c., which, supplemented from those long rows of celery, and with certain yet more nutritious adjuncts from the butcher (a sober, married man, as Mr. Grundy knows, and a very happy contrast to poor "Sammel Cox"), make the soup, so welcome during these winter months, in those same cottage homes.

Now step into my miniature houses of glass. Nearest to the boiler (a cruciform, from Meiklejon of Dalkeith) is my hothouse, about the size of a saloon railway-carriage. I make no attempt, of course, to grow stove-plants; but it is not without its bits of beauty—the silver-leafed Fittonia, the red-veined Gymnostachium (which poor Pearce sent us from Peru); the narrow-leafed Croton, weeping gold; the velvety Gesnera (so named by the great Linnæus after

---

* I cannot write the word without recalling a speech made by a poor old woman in Worcestershire to one of my college companions: "Yes, Mr. Allen, I've had a deal o' trouble. First I lost my sister, and then I lost my pig. But there's one thing I ought to say, and say it I will,—the Lord's been pratty well on my side this winter—for greens!"

his brother botanist, Gesner of Zurich); the bright Poinsettia, with its scarlet spaths; the first batch of Gloxinias, just showing leaf; the few rare ferns, A. Farleyense (not the "big one," awful in Mr. Evans's ears), Cheilanthes elegans, and other gems; the lovely and abundant Eucharis and Pancratium, from which, and from the Stephanotis, on the roof above, many a sweet maid has had her bride's bouquet. But I chiefly use my tiny stove as a propagating and forcing house; and in that central bed of tan, warmed by the pipes below, seeds germinate, bulbs "spindle," grafts "callus," and cuttings strike, with a sure success and speed. Better than all this—I force early strawberries here, which, after giving me intense pleasure by their fragrant beauty, are invaluable in cases where a failing appetite has often longed and craved for them. A good doctor once sent a dozen miles for the same number of berries, and he told me afterwards that his patient " would gladly have paid a pound apiece for them."

From the vinery, which adjoins my stove, and the greenhouse, which completes my " range," I have—beyond the great delight of watching the vines break into leaf, and the fruit develop, and flower, and colour; and beyond the constant refreshment which I find in my plants, my primulas and hyacinths, my roses and geraniums and fuchsias—a far more ample and continuous help in ministering to the sick. A great number of invalids will eat grapes when they can eat nothing else; and several have told me that this fruit was the first thing which they seemed to relish in the earliest stage of their recovery. As for flowers, it is needless to expatiate on the comfort which their brightness and their sweetness bring to the ailing, for all who have ever suffered (and who has not ?) know their cheering influence in the sick-room. "Oh, how I love them!" once sighed a dying girl to me. "I dreamed last night that He stood by them, and said, 'Consider the lilies, how they grow.' I think—I feel sure—there will be flowers in heaven." And these words are carved upon the stone by her grave: "*My Beloved is gone down into His garden, to gather lilies. I am my Beloved's and my Beloved is mine.*"

Let us leave now my crystal palaces, and spend a few minutes in my open ground. A small space,* much smaller than it seems, because the surface rises and falls, and no boundary lines are seen, but full of treasures precious beyond words to me. By lowering here, and by raising there, and by a little thoughtful arrangement of bank and wall and shrub, I have realized a score of cosy nooks and corners, in which I have more privacy, and, as I believe, more pleasure than can be found in your great modern gardens, cleared by the axe, and prepared by spirit-level and line and compass, for a vast geometrical design. There, you see, is our little fernery (I say *our*, because I have an excellent coadjutor, fellow-gardener, and forewoman in my sister Rose); there, as her name reminds me, our bank of roses, on which our critical

---

* The Curate's garden and glass is kept in order by himself, his sister, and his man-of-all-work. Now and then, but from charity more than necessity, a labourer is set on to dig, or an old woman to sweep and weed.

President has smiled his praise; there our rockery,—
our "Switzerland," as we call it, in honour of those
exquisite Alpine plants; and close to Switzerland (let
Pinnock protest as he may), "America" (I made
America myself last autumn with six cart-loads of
peaty soil), with its Andromedas, azaleas, kalmias,
and rhododendrons, bordered with the ericas, roseate
and white, and with that delicious spice-scented
Daphne cneorum! Here and there, as you follow our
tortuous walks, are beds, with evergreens and flowering
shrubs in the centre, and perennial and herbaceous
flowers around, the latter covering them to the grass,
save where, in some few exceptions, you see a vacant
space of some two or three feet in width, devoted in
the spring and summer months to the plants known
as "bedding-outers." There, under my study-
window, which has all the morning sun, the violets
bloom half the year; and there, opposite, close to the
yews, and under the shade of melancholy boughs, the
lilies of the valley scent the vernal air.

There remain two small inclosures which we have not
yet explored. In the first one of these, which we call
our garden of memories, we have, on the right as you
enter, a border of shrubs and flowers, of which every
one was given to us by some dear relation or friend
(you will find that the *Souvenir d'un ami* rose has
been a frequent choice), and many placed there by
the hands which gave. Each has a special history,
and brings its welcome thoughts; each whispers in
the ear that word, which you may see, carved in
Hebrew letters, on the stone before you, with forget-
me-nots around its base, *Mizpah*—"The Lord watch

between me and thee, when we are absent one from another."

On your left is a collection, also very dear to us, of plants, ferns, and flowers, brought from distant places (Scotland, Ireland, Wales), and from many a pleasant home—memorials of our happy wanderings amid the fairest scenes of earth, and reminding us also that the brightest day of every pilgrimage was that which brought us back to—our garden.

The last small plat to which I invite you is our garden of Palestine, wherein we have collected many of the trees and shrubs and flowers which are mentioned in the Holy Scriptures, aware, of course, that in several instances—as, for example, the apple and the juniper trees, the hyssop, the lily, and the rose—our specimens are identical only in name. For this reason we have included both trees and flowers, such as the apricot and the anemone, which, although not mentioned in the Bible, are found in abundance upon the sacred soil, and were probably referred to and intended by words imperfectly translated in our tongue. Here, then, are the trees, the grasses, herbs, fruits, and flowers, consecrated to our ears by Prophet and Psalmist, and by our Lord Himself—the cedar and the cypress, the oak and the elm, the fir-tree, the pine-tree, and the box-tree together, from which, at Christmas, and Easter, and other holy seasons, we "beautify the place of the sanctuary;" there, upon the southward wall, grow the vine, the fig-tree, and the gourd, and, close by, the myrtle and the green bay-tree; and there, where our village brook forms the boundary of my garden, is the tree planted by the water-side,—the willow weeps, as by the rivers of Babylon—the reed is shaken by the wind. The passiflora, protected in winter, has shown in the heat of summer those wondrous emblems of the passion upon that old stone cross. I need make no comment upon these things. There is neither speech nor language, but their voices are heard among them. Indeed, I should fear that I had already sermonized too much, did I not know that your heart is with my heart, and loves these sacred thoughts. How could I be here did I not feel myself with those who forget not Jerusalem in their mirth—with Christian gardeners, who hear "the voice of the Lord God, walking in the garden," and speaking to them, not in wrath, as to the first gardener, of Paradise Lost, but, in all the tenderness of redeeming love, of Paradise Regained.

MY FIRST FIGHT IN THE WARS OF THE ROSES.

MAGPIES were manly, for Jones the Prefect kept one, and guinea-pigs were quite genteel; but we might not even speak of flowers. They were considered to be beneath the dignity of gentlemen who would be nine years of age next birthday. It was quite legitimate to make toffy, and it was honourable to play at horses; but when Simpkins *minimus* bought a fuchsia there was one wild howl of scorn. Entomology had ardent friends : butterflies were extensively impaled on cork; silkworms were openly maintained; cockchafers were diligently harnessed to elegant landaus of walnut-shell, with buttons of bone for wheels; frequent trials of strength and science were very generally encouraged between the various species of the genus beetle, and a terrific duel between a "Soldier" and a "Sailor," which took place in a large pill-box, was the thrilling topic of "the half." There were collections of eggs, shells, seals, and autographs (I myself presented one of the juniors with a unique assortment of the latter, comprising scores of distinguished heroes, from Alfred the Great to Bendigo, and all written, like Dr. Johnson's Dictionary, with a single pen), but not a boy of us dare to bring home a posy. Any such pusillanimous proceeding would infallibly have evoked from our disgusted community those epithets, so awful to the boyish soul, viz., "softy," "nincompoop," and "mollycoddy." We trembled to remember those dark ages when we had loved the wild rose and the honeysuckle, when we had filled our small fists with violets, made golden balls of the cowslip, decked ourselves with daisy-chains, and when we were never weary of the tiny garden which was called our own.

Such was our schoolboy creed. Venus was worshipped with so much devotion that twenty-six of us were in love with the same young lady; Diana was worshipped, by reason of her hunting propensities; Minerva was reverenced; Pomona was adored; but none brought sacrifice to Flora. She was heterodox and excommunicated, a female Bishop Colenso. I rejoice to know that it is no longer so. I rejoice to see and to scent in the small studies at Eton, Harrow, and elsewhere, abundant evidences of a taste which adds so largely and so lastingly to the refinement and happiness of life. I only regret that it was not so in my time; that it was not as evident to us as to our sons that there is no incompatibility between a mental and a muscular, an intellectual and a physical excellence; that the eye and hand which are occupied in training and in tending some beautiful plant are not disabled by that process from making a leg-hit for four; and that of all the capacities which distinguish man from the irrational world, that is surely one of the most noble which teaches him to appreciate the works of God.

Oxford, had she deserved in my case the title of "gentle mother," would have removed the bandage from mine eyes, but, on the contrary, she rather tightened it. We had, it is true, a Professor of Botany, but he might as well have resided at Botany Bay for anything we saw or knew of him. There was a garden too, attached to our college, but nothing was ever sown in it, save wild oats and exhausted "weeds"; and I can only remember a single window which was beautified with flowering plants, and this "because" (as I was assured on inquiry, though I was quite unable to understand the inference) "the occupier was going over to Rome." We went regularly enough to the Commemoration Flower Shows, but it was something which Mr. Turner would himself allow to be more attractive than his grand pelargoniums, which took us there in our dandy suits. There was a brightness even brighter than the glowing flowers, there were tints more roseate than the Rose's self, which won our earnest gaze. Very different were our exclamations and inquiries then as we entered the Exhibition tents to those which we utter now. Instead of "Look at that fern!" "What lovely orchids!" "Who has won the cup?" it was, "Have you seen little Jack Thompson's sister? a screamer, sir, a perfect screamer!" (the dissyllable "screamer" was meant to indicate a maiden of peerless beauty), or, "Did you ever see such a dear little duck as that in the lavender bonnet?"

FIRST FIGHT IN THE WARS OF THE ROSES. 205

I was roused at last from my slumber, "awaking with a start," like Byron dreaming of his child; and I emerged as suddenly from darkness to light as a midday express from a tunnel. Having small belief in instantaneous conversions, I must nevertheless confess that on this occasion I met with a missionary, who immediately induced me to acknowledge and renounce the ignorance of many years, and voluntarily and heartily to enrol myself in a brotherhood, of which up to this moment I knew nothing, the happy brotherhood of Florists. Many a glad summer have I passed, and many a high festival have I kept since then, with that most worshipful company, but I ever remember vividly, as though it were yesternight, the hour and scene,

"A goodly place, a goodly time,"

when once again my dear love of flowers, dormant for so many dreary years, bloomed in my thankful heart. I know the spot to a yard where one summer's eve I met the missionary who revived that love, and the missionary's name was—*Rose.* *

It stopped, it startled me. Did you ever, my reader, in early childhood betroth yourself to some tiny damsel, solemnly designate her your "little wifey," and swear eternal love? And was it your destiny again to meet her, after an absence of some half-score years, no longer a child, with traces of jam on her small pinafore, but—

* See p. 108.

> "A daughter of the gods,
> Divinely fair, and most divinely tall,"

reasserting her ancient sway, with such a resistless majesty as took your breath away? If so, you will remember, mingled with that strange surprise and happiness, a feeling of regret and shame that you should have so long forsaken and almost forgotten your first, and, as you now confess, your last and only love. It was thus with this Rose and me. " Young man," that Rose seemed to say, " behold one whom you have despised, deserted! Behold one to whom, in days when it was your chief, unwearying gladness to wander among the flowers and love them, you plighted your early troth. You forsook me, and for what? At first, for sparrow-nets and baiting-needles, for skates and pony-whips, for bats and footballs. Latterly, for your hunters, your flirtations, your London tailors, Ah! you blush, you repent, you return. Well, then, I will be generous; I will forget all, save our old affection. Henceforth be faithful, and in your fidelity you shall find a purer, surer happiness than any you have known since you left me to blush, unseen by any but the gardener, and to waste my sweetness on the bees and butter-flies."

I went down on my knees (metaphorically I mean, not upon the gravel, for I was arrayed in my " extra-fine, double-milled, evening pants" at £2 6s. the pair, and could not afford the genuflection), I went down, and acknowledged my transgressions. I re-newed my broken vows to Flora; I swore a lasting allegiance to the Royal rose; and I have performed my promise as faithfully as the great Lord Bateman himself, when "he wowed a wow, and kept it strong."

To speak less fancifully and more closely to the plain facts, I became from that summer's evening an enthusiastic rose-grower. I dreamed about roses that summer's night, and next morning hurried over my early breakfast that I might canter to the nearest nursery. A nursery! I should as soon have thought, twenty-four hours before, of visiting a nursery as a Jew of spending his day at a pork-butcher's, or a wooden-legged man of deriving enjoyment from a protracted sojourn in a boot-and-shoe shop! And now I was positively bewildered with admiration. I should have liked to transfer the whole stock to my garden, and did in my ignorance suggest the immediate removal of a portion, to the surprised amusement of the owner, who suggested that, as I might wish the trees to survive for another season, November would be a wiser date. Meantime he would cut me a bouquet to soothe me in my disappointed impatience. And I carried a bunch of roses home on horseback about the size of a tree-peony, scornfully declining to notice the sarcastic inquiry of a friend, whom I met on the road,—"Holloa, John Thomas! whatever are you doing, away from the back of the carriage?"

Autumn brought the catalogues, of which, if my memory is true, there were at that time four only, emanating from Messrs. Rivers, Paul, Lane, and Wood. Ah! had I studied my books at Oxford with half the zest with which I devoured these catalogues, what pre-eminence I might have won! I read, re-read, compared, and annotated those pages until my sisters asked sneeringly, "What could I see in those stupid lists?" and prophesied an early softening of my brain. The youngest, I remember, to whom in an incautious moment I had exhibited my Masonic apron, "felt sure that they came from that horrid lodge," and sniffed at them as though they smelt of sulphur. But to me, nevertheless, it was and has been from that day to this a never-failing amusement to study, as in a gallery, these portraits by different artists of Queen Rosa and her suite—a gratification like that which lovers feel as they gaze upon the likeness of their absent darling.

At last, and after as careful deliberation as though I had been some fond mamma who was engaged in choosing husbands for her daughters, with all the swells of Rotten Row to pick from, I made my "purchaser's own selection," and sent my order to a neighbouring nurseryman, with quite as high an idea of its importance as though I were raising him to the peerage. My conviction was that no demand of similar magnitude (two dozen rose-trees!) had been previously made by any amateur, and that, when they were added to my existing stock of ten, they would be, as Mr. Wombwell says of his menagerie, "a magnificent and unrivalled collection." I knew not then how the rose-lover's appetite grows with that it feeds on; I foresaw not the day, when with 1,500 trees I should be sending my plate, like a distended schoolboy, for "just a small slice more."

November, the much maligned—for when do

hounds run better, or when are rose-trees transplanted more successfully?—November brought me one of those matted packages which we florists love so well. There is excitement in unpacking one's first tailed-coat, first gun, first pair of "tops;" but it is transitory, and does not return; whereas the gladness of opening those big bundles and robust hampers fades not, but is a joy for ever. My gardener and I surveyed the under-gardener jealously as he bore our treasure from the carrier's cart, keenly watching, as some mother and mother-in-law might watch the minutest action of a new nursemaid, permitted to carry, for the first time, His Royal Highness the baby. No sooner had we reached the garden-house than, wildly regardless of the expense, recklessly forgetful of Miss Edgeworth's "Waste not, Waste not"— wherein, you may remember, an economical youth produces, at an archery meeting, a piece of string which he had saved, and wins the first prize in a canter — I rushed, open-knifed, at my prostrate package, anxiously as an archæologist at the last new thing in mummies. One by one, the tall clean standards were uplifted, tenderly and delicately, lest harm be done to branch or fibrous root; and those parchment "tallies," which always twist and curl themselves into the most inconvenient positions, like worms who dislike the hook, were read with as much enthusiastic interest as though the trees were in their fullest bloom. "That's the rose we saw at Mr. So-and-So's." "Hear what Mr. Rivers says of this;" and out comes the little red book. "That's the bloom painted in Mr. Paul's work," &c., &c.

And then we started in procession for the rosarium, I and my gardener bearing our bundles as proudly as the Lictors bore the fasces of old, and the rear being brought up by our *aide-de-camp* with a wheelbarrow of rich, fine soil. Nothing could well surpass in solemnity the dignified air of our demeanour, grandly and yet calmly majestic, as of men who essay a most momentous exploit, but feel no fear. Had we been selected by a committee of crowned heads to turn the first sod of some new, grand, universal railway, or had we been conquering heroes about to plant our standard on some height or citadel just won from flying foes, our countenances could not have shone with a more complete satisfaction.

And now, upon these rosy recollections, like the shadow of a cloud over a summer garden, there sweeps a sudden gloom. Those flowers, so loved, so reverenced, tended so carefully, watched so patiently, bloom no more save in the loyal memory of those who honour " auld lang syne." " I came to the place of my youth, and I said, ' The roses of my youth, where are they ? ' And Echo answered, ' Oh, bother you and the roses of your youth ; we don't grow such rubbish nowadays ! ' " Ah, thoughtless, not to say ungentlemanly Echo ! *Nimium ne crede colori.* Despise not those roses of the past, for, twenty years hence, it will be with these as with them ; and some vulgar upstart of an Echo will inform posterity that thy vaunted blooms were— rubbish. Be satisfied, and more than satisfied, with that which is before thee. Thankful contentment is the fresh, full spring whence flows the florist's never-failing joy; and happiest he who bends to admire the commonest, the lowliest flower, the wee, modest daisy, rather than not admire at all.

Continuing my retrospect, I am now reminded of a most impressive epoch, my first *début* as an exhibitor of roses. For I, like Norval, "had heard of battles," and the time came when my father, like Mr. Norval, senior, found it quite impossible "to keep his only son, myself, at home," or prevent me from sallying forth to fight in the wars of the roses. The Reverend Jones, my neighbour, had long maintained an absolute monarchy at all our country flower-shows, and it was time to hurl the tyrant from his throne. I am afraid that I was jealous of Jones. To see him smiling and purring over victorious roses, surrounded by no end of pretty girls; to hear the latter praising and extolling Jones, as though he had made the roses himself, was rather more than I could stand. He was a formidable foe; but I felt myself aggrieved, like the old lady's parrot, and thirsted for Jones's gore. You know the story of the old lady's parrot— how he escaped from his cage, and wandering into the inn yard opposite, was immediately attacked by a gigantic raven; and how his alarmed mistress, espying the battle from afar, rushed to the rescue, caught up her bleeding favourite, and was astounded to hear his plucky expostulations, "*Set me down, missus, set me down. Big brute has broke my leg. I'll have a go at him. I'll have a go at him.*" So with me; if Jones broke not my leg, he metaphorically trod upon my most sensitive corn, and I determined to "*have a go at him.*"

I went into training forthwith. I studied the catalogues more closely than ever, and added a hundred trees to my stock. I remembered, with the liveliest and most unchristian gratification, that Jones showed his roses in ginger-beer bottles, and that Mr. Lane, of Berkhampstead, had kindly explained to me all the details of his exhibition boxes, and had lent me a zinc tube for a pattern. Oh, would I not astonish my friend, and punish him for his execrable disloyalty in sticking the Flower Queen into a pop-bottle!

There is excitement in the small bosom of the schoolboy, who has just returned for his Christmas holidays, and is to hunt on the morrow. He roams restlessly upstairs and downstairs, from his bedroom —where, attired in his new "riding pants," he has been surveying himself for the fourteenth time—to the stable, where abides the jumping cob, and where he never wearies of hearing from the groom that he "needn't turn 'im from nothing." And won't he astonish Master Brown, his schoolmate and neighbour, who is sure to be out "on that one-eyed brute of a pony"; and won't he gallop past Puncher maximus, who has thrashed him liberally during the last half, if he can only catch him in some dirty lane! He cracks his hunting-whip in the hall; he "who-ops" in the shrubberies; and, finally, retires to dream that he has "pounded" all the field over an extra-sized canal, and that as he flies over its sullen waters, the head of Puncher maximus bobs up, and fixes on him a look of envy and despair.

And thus did I, on the eve of my first Rose-Show,

stray feverishly indoors and out. Now in my garden, gazing reproachfully at those roses which were not in sufficient bloom, as though they had done it to spite me, and trying to induce a premature development, until I cracked their petals and spoiled them; and now, under cover, filling my zinc tubes, picking out the best moss for my boxes, and writing correct cards of the names and species of the roses which were to race for the cup. All was in readiness when, as the daylight fell, I took a last lingering survey of my pets. There was a *Baronne Prevost*, I remember, which I rather flattered myself would make Jones gasp; a *Countess Molé* of such ample proportions as would have won her praise in Brobdignag; and a grand specimen of *Las Casas*, which we then accounted to be a noble rose, not criticizing in those days so keenly as in these, an "eye" about the size of a shilling! With blooms of this calibre, tastefully disposed, I fully hoped to bring disgrace on Jones; and I saw him that night in my broken slumbers, bringing out of his usual hamper twenty-four small and sullied roses, sticking them, without any regard to size or colour, in the ginger-beer bottles, to which I have previously referred, and of course miserably defeated.

There was no need next morning for the small bits of gravel, which my faithful gardener threw up to my bedroom window, for I was nearly dressed when the summons came, and in my garden at four a.m. My reader, if you have never seen roses when, refreshed by those welcome dews which flow "from the cool cisterns of the midnight air," they awake in the soft splendour of the rising sun, you have yet to see them in their glory. It seemed a cruel wrong to decapitate them, and yet why should they be as lost to the general public as though they "sprang in deserts where no men abide"? *Il faut souffrir pour être* admired; and, moreover, Jones's time was come.

We reached the place of exhibition, my gardener and I, at least three hours before there was the slightest necessity, and a considerable time before the doors were opened of the hall in which the show was held. There was no trace to be seen of our adversary, and a lively hope began to gleam in my ungenerous breast that possibly he had come to grief. Had a special messenger arrived to inform us that the Reverend Jones's market-cart had broken down abruptly, and that his roses were strewed over the king's high-road, I fear that I should not have experienced that large amount of earnest sympathy which is due to a clergyman in distress. Nay, I blush to confess that a vision of beetles nibbling at Jones's favourite blooms presented itself to my imagination, and that I did not repel it, as I ought to have done.

Communicating with the hall were several anterooms, in which we prepared our flowers for exhibition; and just as, after a most elaborate and careful arrangement, I emerged from one of these, proudly bearing my precious freight before me—oh! what do you think that, to my intense dismay and horror, I confronted in that wretched lobby? *Jones*, with a brand-new box, the facsimile of my own, zinc tubes, green moss, and everything in the highest style of art! We met face to face, like Box and Cox with their two tea-trays, muttered a mutual "How d'ye do?" which meant, "What business have you here?" glared at each other's roses, and separated. But, alas! in that brief survey what did I behold! The brute had actually got a *Baronne Prevost*, beating mine by half an inch in diameter, several roses which I had never even seen, and, to crown all, a yellow *Noisette*, which I knew would be the envy and admiration of every pretty girl in the show.

Three hours afterwards that show was open to the British public, and my cup of misery brimmed over when my enemy met me in the middle of the hall, and remarked to me patronizingly, before a crowd of people, "They've disqualified you for extra foliage, or I really believe that you would have come in *third!*"

SOME CORNISH GARDENS.

THE GARDEN AT LAMORRAN.

IN small lodgings at Truro, that I might be near my work (addresses and sermons daily), I had a pleasant proof of that genial sympathy which animates our floral guild. My little parlour, which commanded a near and full, but somewhat monotonous, view of the scaffolding of the new cathedral, was brightened and perfumed by three fresh blooms of Maréchal Niel Rose, sent home as the first produce of the tree by a lady resident in Truro, unknown to me even by name. And then came a box containing some grand specimens of roses, which contrasted beautifully with the golden Maréchals, and which, though they had travelled from Guernsey to Caunton and thence to Truro, still retained their full size and symmetry and their deep rich crimson tints. They were the first flowers I had seen of Climbing Charles Lefebvre, and the description which the donor, Mr. E. Peters, of The Gardens, Somerset Terrace, Guernsey, gives of the parent makes my mouth water (rose-water, of course) to possess it. The blooms were cut, he informs me, from a tree which is grown in a large span-roofed greenhouse, and makes a growth of from fifteen to twenty feet, flowering freely. *Gaudete sodales!* Surely a wall covered with Charles Lefebvre and Maréchal Niel in the middle of April will leave nothing for the rosarian to desire, except a robust climbing Marie Baumann with flowers as white as snow.

So always, and go where he may, the gentle gardener shall find genial friends, and, though he has left his apron at home, shall be recognized and welcomed by the craft, just as we freemasons realize our brotherhood, however far we have wandered from our lodge. This I found to be specially certified, as regards the former fraternity, in those fair gardens of the duchy of Cornwall which it was my happiness to see; and good reason had I to endorse the statement of the old historian, Diodorus Siculus : " The natives of that part of Britain which is called Belerium, to wit, the Land's End, are not only hospitable, but civilized in their living." Accordingly, when I had finished my work, and, setting forth on a bright, sunny morning for a holiday, with the glad conviction that I had earned it, had strolled for a couple of miles on the banks of the Fal—vessels from Norway unloading their great beams of timber on the right, and great bushes of golden furze and silver blackthorn showing on the left—I saw on the opposite bank of the ferry at Malpas (pronounced, with a supreme disdain of its French appearance, Mopus) a brother, whom I hardly knew beyond the repute which he has won in the floral world, waving a preliminary welcome, to be completed, on my landing, with hand and heart.

He drove me through the woods of Tregothnan, which must be charming indeed to sight and to scent when the honeysuckles, which climb to the very top of the trees, are in flower and fragrance, and which were charming then in their early leafage, and with their primrose carpet below. And he showed me Tregothnan itself, the stately house and spacious gardens, with the camellias growing freely and flowering abundantly, as climbers on the walls and as shrubs in the open air, much as you see them in Southern France and Italy. Laurels also grown into great trees, and on either side of the broad drives and walks, with a wide margin of grass intervening, the rhododendrons! Then, for the first time, I saw these trees in their glory, beautiful pyramids, fifteen to twenty feet in height, and covered from base to crown with great trusses of white, and roseate, and crimson, and purple flowers. The taller trees of the shrubberies made an admirable background, and here and there the snowy blossoms of the cherry a most pleasing contrast. There is a grand old cork tree and many fine conifers, perhaps the best specimen of Torreya myristica in this country, and the most amiable Amabilis I ever saw.

Then, if I may diverge a few hundred yards from the garden, we saw the famous "Devons," small in stature, but thoroughbred, solemn, graceful in demeanour, as though they traced their pedigree to the sacred bulls of the Brahmin, faultless as to symmetry and condition also; in short, just such as you would expect to see in the yards of the Lord of Tregothnan, acknowledged, as he is, to be one of the best, if not the best, of our judges and breeders. As we gazed on these beautiful animals, and as they gazed on us, I became suddenly self-convicted of a life-long mistake and injustice. I had always considered that our old friend Homer displayed a melancholy proof of his defective vision, and illustrated the statement, "Aliquando bonus dormitat Homerus," when he called the belles of the Iliad ox-eyed, $βo\hat{ω}πις$, but as I looked into the large, bright, expressive orbs of these pretty Devons I began to think that the old gentleman was right.

Then, as we walked from the park to the rectory, my companion showed me, one mile to our right, the supposed site of the tomb of St. Geraint (Gerentius), and told me how, during the excavations of the antiquarian, they found withered bunches of flowers supposed to have been placed, as we place them now, in the grave, and how he collected the seed and sowed them in his garden, and these sleeping beauties woke up after a trance of thirteen centuries, to wit, since the days of King Arthur, and produced the same wild flowers, which ever since then, and I know not how long before, have sprung from Cornish soil.

Believing in Eden as thoroughly as though I had seen it, as undoubtedly as though no elegant and clever sceptic, lighting his cigarette, after a costly meal, before the excitement of his rubber, had ever sneered at my simple faith; believing that our love of horticulture and our happiness in a garden are reminiscences of our first glorious home, and longings to reproduce it; liking those gardens best which seem to instruct us most convincingly how, by a great love and a long labour, we may change Paradise Lost to Paradise Regained, in which refined taste, and skilful culture, and continuous work are patiently striving to eliminate that which is noxious and unsightly, and to replace it with all things pleasant to the eye and good for food, I shall never forget that "goodly place and goodly time"—the garden at Lamorran—and the joyous hours which passed so quickly there. It is indeed " a garden wild, but not without a plan," and that plan is to combine and blend Nature with art, imports and home produce, so to diversify and surprise without incongruous or too sudden change, that the eye of the visitor should never weary, and that his steps, though upward, should never tire; but that increase of appetite should grow with that it fed on, and sigh, with the French lover, *trop n'est pas assez.*

And it is marvellous to see, and all negligent gardeners should be shown or told, how much a master-mind, with only one fellow-workman—not an artist—can realize and maintain. There seemed to be in that extensive hill-side garden not only everything which we gardeners love the most, trees, evergreen and deciduous, notably the Sikkim rhododendrons, the named hybrids raised by the owner, such as the lovely Lady of the Lake and Rose of Falmorren; graceful palms, such as Chamærops excelsa; also Paulownias and Bambusas; conifers in their full grandeur, so happy that they grew self-sown; and I noticed a robust young Pinus insignis which had started business on his own account, and was thriving prosperously; not only are there flowers of all denominations—alpine, herbaceous, or shrubs, from bulbs, vernal, æstival, autumnal, and hybernal, lilies from minimum to maximum (giganteum twelve feet high), for Mr. Boscawen was one of the first who grew them *al fresco;* not only to this charming site, which commands exquisite views of the river below, and of the oak woods beyond, and to this genial climate, in which the Lapageria flourishes on his walls, and the standard peach tree fruits in the open, has he brought all things bright and beautiful, but he has arrayed them with a consummate grace of congruity; there he holds his own against all comers—slugs, rabbits, hares, outlying deer, ungenial seasons; and there he has established, and long may he enjoy, the most perfect example of a wild garden, which, as I believe, is to be found in England.*

THE GARDEN AT PORTHGWIDDEN.

I would observe of Cornish gardens generally, that, favoured as they are, in their glens and glades and on their sunny slopes, by climate and culture, nature and art, they present a striking contrast, which much enhances their beauty, with the moorlike and monotonous scenery of the country through which you pass to see them. A Cambridge don, inviting Dr. Whewell to visit him in Cornwall, is said to have given to that illustrious scholar this direction: "When

* Both he and his brother, Lord Falmouth, have since died

you get into the county, keep going on till you see some trees—those trees are mine." And the late Bishop of Exeter, who had a habit of speaking as he thought and quoting as he spoke, used to remark to his neighbours, "Your shrubs are trees, but your trees are scrubs." You will find glorious conifers fifty feet in height, but you will not find timber trees. And now, alas! those gracious gifts by which the generous earth more than repaid the sterility of her surface by the abundance of her precious ores within, have lost their power to compensate; and when I asked why there was silence and desolation around the mines, and only here and there a chimney smoked, the answer which I received was this, "They cannot compete with foreign imports."

Looking down upon the estuary, from which the Fal flows into the sea, commanding lovely views of both, of the former to the left, and of the latter as you look to the right beyond Falmouth, "a havyn very notable and famose," as Leland writes, "and in a manner the most principale of al Britayne," the garden at Porthgwidden, with its pleasant paths, conducting you from the fair home above to the banks and bathing-place below, amid rare trees, and shrubs, and flowers, gracefully arranged and tended with skilful care, is one of the most charming of our cultured grounds, reminding us of Spencer's words—

"It was a chosen plot of fertile land,
    Amid wild waves set like a little nest,
    As if it had by Nature's cunning hand
        Been choicely pickèd out from all the rest."

A list of its treasures would be longer than that which Leporello made of the ladies who were specially admired by his master, and I will only mention, to justify my quotation from the poet, that whereas the aucubas which I had left at home were cut down to the soil, and their blackened leaves resembled the remnants of a fire, here they were golden pillars ten feet high, and covered with scarlet berries; and the Embothrium coccineum, which, with its vivid crimson flowers and glossy foliage, is one of the most beautiful of all plants, and which, Paxton tells us in his "Botanical Dictionary," attains a height of three feet, was here a fine, tall garden shrub, with an abundance of healthy buds.

Taking a preliminary view of the conservatory from the drawing-room, my gaze was riveted by a gem of purest ray serene, which fascinated me as a new star fascinates an astronomer, or a new hunter an undergraduate. What could it be? Nine heads of beautiful bloom, the flowers white, of exquisite purity, five inches across! It was Rhododendron Aucklandi, and dear ever since has that flower been to my memory, not only as a florist, but as a teacher of humility. For now, whenever I meet with one of those objectionable brethren, who think they know everything and possess everything which is to be learned or procured in floriculture, I make a point of suggesting, " Of course you have Rhododendron Aucklandi " (which, of course, they haven't); and, whatever they say or show, I keep wishing they could see "*that* plant," until they hate the whole Rhododendron family, and are evidently thinking that if I were relegated to the Land's End, to contemplate the flower in question, they would not be annoyed by my abrupt departure—only detaining me to ask, "Where can we get it?" and receiving the answer, "Can't say." I have sought, where I thought I should surely find, at the birthplace of those lovely rhododendrons, the Princesses Royal, Alexandria, Alice, Helena, the Duchesses of Edinburgh and Teck, the Countess of Haddington, and the untitled, but admirable, Taylori and Veitchianum; but when I announced the object of my desire (with the sure confidence of a man who asks at Gunter's for an ice) "I want a plant of Rhododendron Aucklandi," the reply which I received, though it was less curtly and more courteously expressed, was in effect this, then "want must be your master." *

And "there was a round pond, and a pretty pond too," quite filled with the flowers, deliciously fragrant, of the Aponogeton. The plant had been placed, in the first instance, and in accordance with the suggestive meaning of its name—that is, "near to water" —upon a pile of stones which rose just above the pool. There it existed for some time, but that was all. There was no development of vigour, no efflorescence. One memorable day, a boy, playful, impulsive, quaint in imagination, quick in action, was wandering in this delightful garden, accompanied by a pair of those idle hands for which we know that a large assortment of mischief is always kept in readiness. He beheld the Aponogeton, and whether he

* I finally obtained it from the Dublin Botanical Gardens, but I could not persuade it to bloom.

despised it as a failure, or whether from its isolated and prominent position it suggested that fascinating, because somewhat perilous, diversion which is known as "duck and drake," or whether, as I have intimated, he was impelled by a spirit of mere mischief, I cannot say, but the boy began to bowl at the flower-pot, and he very soon bowled it over. And now, imploring all parents and guardians who may have lively lads about them to keep these chronicles out of their sight, lest they should consider it their vocation to shy at every pot they see, I have to record the unhoped and happy consequences of that *bouleversement*. The Aponogeton, thus hurled from its exalted place, and finding itself in low water, at once began, like many a noble mind which has been lethargized by inaction and roused by some sudden shock, to make sweet uses of adversity, displayed all its latent powers, established itself in a business, which grew and prospered in all its branches, and steadily accumulated a floating capital, which literally filled the surrounding banks.

Passing from the Upper to the Lower Houses, from the Lords, or rather the Ladies, to the Commons, that is, the general range of glass, we come first to an arrangement which may be commended as a model, all the more worthy of imitation because it has now been tested for a period of thirty years. The range consists of (1) a forcing pit, forty-two by eight feet, divided into three compartments, in which pot vines, melons, cucumbers, &c., are grown in quick succession, with a healthful vigour of foliage and fruitage which I never saw surpassed. Then (2), with a walk intervening, there is an orchid house of the same length, ten feet wide, in two compartments, containing a choice collection of these lovely luxuries, which are beyond my exchequer and experience, and of which I only remember Odontoglossum Alexandræ, and amid countless beautiful Cypripediums, hirsutum, Lowi, and niveum. On the north side of the orchid house there is (3) a row of frames for striking, to which heat may be given at pleasure. The entire cost was £160, and the consumption of fuel is about nine tons of culm (at 14s. per ton) per annum.

But I have made special mention of this range of houses, of which the reader who possesses *The Journal of the Royal Horticultural Society* will find a full account illustrated in vol. vii., part i., because, though the heating is admirable, the chief source of its complete success is the constant supply of fresh air. Canon Phillpotts maintains and proves that the most perfect system of heating will fail without good ventilation day and night, and that the air of plant houses should be in direct proportion to the light, the moisture, and the heat. At the same time, care must be taken that the temperature is not lowered too much or too suddenly by the admission of external air, while, on the other hand, it must not be dried by artificial heat. To obviate this difficulty there is an air chamber between the two buildings, from which several small drains open into the pits, &c., six inches above the floor, with gratings about six inches square of perforated zinc. From these a constant supply of fresh air in small and broken quantities arrives, so that there is no strong draught, and this passing over the surface of the pipes under which it enters loses its chill, while the open troughs supply it with water. This introduction of good air has been continued without intermission since the range was erected in the year 1850.

After recording, something more than a quarter of a century ago, his first satisfaction with this excellent system in the journal to which I have referred, the writer concludes: "Such successful results can only be expected where the gardener not merely understands, but loves his business. It is but common justice to add that I have the good fortune to be so assisted, and that I highly value the care, attention, and zeal with which my plans have been carried out." Though there have been changes since then, the worthy Canon has still the same cause for congratulation, for in horticulture, as in all things else, a good master attracts good servants, and keeps them. When men are united by mutual appreciation, not only of the beautiful, but of the dutiful also, that brotherly intercourse should never cease.

THE GARDEN AT PENJERRICK.

I saw yet one more lovely garden, some think the loveliest in Cornwall, Penjerrick, a deep long glen of beauty, from its peaceful home to the sea, rich in trees and shrubs, coniferous, floriferous, evergreen, deciduous, rarely seen in any part of England, and nowhere else in a more prosperous condition. In these sheltered vales of the western coast we seem to have our nearest approximation to the climate and vegetation of the Mediterranean shores, and though the sky and sea are not so intensely blue, and we miss the Olive, and the Orange, and the Lemon; the queen of flowers in those garments of Cloth of Gold, which even royalty cannot afford to wear in this land of smoke and shower; the Bougainvilleas glabra and spectabilis, so charming in their mauve and rosy-purple splendour upon the white walls of Monaco; we are, nevertheless, reminded by the Paulownia, Wigandia, Araucaria brasiliensis; by that blue bloom which reveals health and happiness on the branches of the Pinaceæ, and declares the Thuja to be an Arbor-vitæ, and not, as too often in our northern gardens, an Arbor-mortis; by the "Big Laurel," the Magnolia; by Camellias, Azaleas, Pittospora, Veronicas; by flowers, such as Geraniums, Cinerarias, and Salvias, blooming through the winter; by these, and many other proofs that horticulture likes both protection (from cold winds) and free trade (in sunshine); we are reminded of the Riviera.

And I saw at Penjerrick the best specimens which I have met with in England of the Eucalyptus, but they had not, and they never will have in this country, any signs of the wonderful luxuriant growth which they develop in a genial clime. Even in Southern France, where in fifteen years they assume the proportions of timber trees (witness the specimen on the Quai de Massena, at Nice), they showed in many instances manifest signs of punishment after the winters of 1879–80, and there is no more hope of their successful acclimatization with us than that the Mammoth Tree of California, the Wellingtonia gigantea, will ever attain the dimensions of that specimen, of which some of us saw the outer bark (eighteen inches thick) set up in the Crystal Palace, Sydenham, and which was destroyed by the fire in 1866.

Fields of asparagus surprised me as I drew near to Penzance, and a long train of trucks laden with broccoli was just leaving the station for London. Many thousand tons of this vegetable and of early potatoes are annually sent from this terminus. The asparagus is ready about a fortnight in advance of our general crop, but the earlier and larger produce from Versailles, Dijon, &c., materially reduces the amount of profit. I may be misguided by prejudice or palate, but I like our English asparagus, properly grown, not too thickly, well manured and salted, and boiled by some person with brains, much more than the great white batons which are sent to us from France.

I went, of course, to the Land's End, well knowing that if I failed to do so, I should be told in tones of contemptuous pity, on my return home, that I had thrown away an opportunity which might never recur of witnessing one of the most magnificent, &c., &c., and I saw "The Last Inn in England" announced on the sign of the small hotel at Sennen as I went, and "The First Inn in England" on the other side as I returned, and I inspected the Logan Stone, of which it was said that, though a child could move it, no human power could dislodge, until one Goldsmith, a relation of the poet and a lieutenant in the Royal Navy, not believing in impossibilities, and remembering, it may be, the announcement made by Archimedes, that if he had a lever long enough, and a fulcrum strong enough, he could move the world, came ashore with a boat's crew, and, with a certain amount of engineering science and an unlimited amount of muscle and pluck, he dislodged the Logan. Whereupon such a commotion was raised in the district, as when the silversmiths at Ephesus were perturbed in spirit because their craft was in danger, and though this was an afterthought, their goddess was insulted, that the young sailor was severely reprimanded by the authorities, ordered to replace, and did replace, the stone. And then, it is gratifying to know, he made a virtuous resolve that nothing should induce him to contract a habit of upsetting Logan Stones, and he kept it to his dying day.

I saw the white gulls hovering around the great granite rocks of our Land's End and admiring their wives, who were detained at home on urgent private affairs, and for once in an excursive life was allowed to enjoy an interesting view without that chattering abomination called a guide. No one bored me with statements which I knew as well as he; no one came to explain the difference between a kittiwake and a scissor-bill and expected a shilling; no one pressed me to purchase blurred, grimy, thirty-second-rate photographs, conchological specimens, or lemonade. I turned my face from the kittiwakes towards home.

THE SPRING GARDEN AT BELVOIR.

THERE are interesting analogies between a delightful holiday and a good dinner, between the refreshments of the mind and the body. Both must be approached with a keen appetite, and there is no appetite so powerful in its appreciations as that which is produced by work. Both should be enjoyed with companions whose taste are congenial and whose friendship is sincere. In both there should be some special excellence as to the quality and the preparation of the food.

With these adjuncts, after anxious and continuous labour with friends " whose hearts are of each other sure," I went on the 18th of March, a bright and balmy day, to see that which I believe to be at these presents the most beautiful garden in all England! It has been my happy privilege to visit many a fair ground and goodly heritage between the Border and the Land's End; I have admired in many a pleasant plot those tasteful and skilful combinations of Nature and art which are not to be found in other lands, even where climate and scenery are far more favourable than ours; but Belvoir in its vernal loveliness excels them all!

There are, of course, many gardens more extensive, having a longer succession and a more varied display of beauty, such as Mons. Dognin's glorious grounds at Cannes, overlooking the Mediterranean, or those of the Duke of Buccleuch at Drumlanrig, but as a spring garden, to be visited in March and April, I claim for Belvoir a reginal (if I were a Roman Catholic I should say a papal) supremacy. The position is perfect—sunny slopes, " green and of mild declivity," or steep and stony, suggesting alpine plants and pathways, with grand old trees, evergreen and deciduous, over which, as you walk on the higher ranges of the gardens, you see the lake beyond, and through, which as you wander below, the picturesque towers of the castle.

The arrangement of the beds, banks, groups is perfect also; colour just where it is most effective, of every hue, but always in congruity; no gaudy glare to frizzle your eye-lashes; no sensational contrasts, which seem to say, " Now, did you ever?" but an exquisite freshness, brightness, unity, repose. With the exception of a brilliant crimson rhododendron, who, I must say, gave me the idea of having, in the parlance of our day, " a good deal of side on," though he was only there on sufferance as an old inhabitant of that part of the garden before the spring flowers came, I did not see a flower or shrub which could have found a more happy home.

And, *apropos* of arrangements and felicitous disposals, there was uppermost that day in my garden thoughts the glad conviction that the right man was in the right place at Belvoir. I remember a general disappointment and lamentation when Mr. Ingram did not succeed his father in the royal gardens at Windsor, and we, his friends and brethren, murmured in our tents; but now the winter of our discontent is not only over, but made glorious summer when we go to Belvoir and see in that fair scene a work which he could not have achieved even in the beautiful home and under the gracious encouragements of our beloved Queen.

Belvoir était toujours belle voir—ever beautiful—in its stately site upon its wooded hills, but the gardens (always excepting the vegetable kingdom of eight acres, walled round) were comparatively small when Mr. Ingram went to them. Gradually, year after year, by an amount of persevering labour, done by his own staff, which few would have faced, with an occasional remonstrance from his kind and generous employer, the duke, "I suppose you won't be satisfied until you get to Knipton" (a village about three miles away), he has developed his plans, carted countless tons of stone and soil up the steeps, cleared his ground, dug and planted, turned the sombre grove into a glowing garden, and "made the desert smile."

What flowers does he grow? All those which come to us in the sweet spring-tide, and having a natural grace and aptitude (not to dwell upon their delicious fragrance), which is not to be seen in our summer bedding-out. The viola and the primulas, in all their infinite varieties; anemones, brilliant as a guardsman's jacket, or white as his helmet's plume; hyacinths, in their size, and scent, and brightness, as happy as though they were in Holland; the narcissus, bearing its beautiful head, like its namesake, when he admired himself reflected in the fountain, but without his fatal conceit; sheets of myosotis, arabis, and aubrietia, the latter from selected seed, and notably large and good; the tulip, holding up its golden chalice for a shower.

Charming contrasts! Deep blue scillas glowing here and there amid the white arabis; the silver leaf of the euonymus, intermixed with the roseate flowers of erica carnea; the scarlet anemones, rising out from a patch of forget-me-nots. Novelties! That is, to me. A pale pink aubrietia from Mount Athos; Chionodoxa Luciliæ, an exquisite little starry flower, blue, with white centre; a deep rose double primula, of which I forget the name; Azara microphylla, a shrub with yellow flowers, giving forth a strong perfume, exactly like vanilla, and, as these flowers are much visited by bees, Mr. Ingram anticipated a new delight for epicures in his "Vanilla Honey." Olearia Hosti, a white flowering shrub; *cum multis aliis*, of which I have no record.

Which was the most beautiful flower of all? Saxifraga ligulata, first introduced into this country (so Paxton tells us) from Nepaul in 1821, with its great, round, glossy leaves, and its beautiful bunches of rosy blooms, it was certainly the belle of the season at Belvoir. I shall never forget my first sight of it, forming the central line of a large bed, surrounded by dark purple hyacinths and other lovely handmaids, but far eclipsing them all. Mr. Ingram thought that he had in Saxifraga Schraderi a *debutante* for next spring, who would be even more admired than her sister.

At the foot of the slopes the Aponogeton (Cape Pondweed) raises its fragrant white flowers out of a small pool.* Water was discovered in the gardens at Belvoir (though some who read this may not believe it) by a man walking with a forked stick in his hand on the top of the slopes. As he went slowly on, holding the stick just above the surface of the ground, the presence of water below affected him by some process of an electric nature, and caused the fork of the stick to turn upward. As a multitude of witnesses can be heard, and the water is at this moment flowing down the hill, I do not advise doubtful persons to "back" their unbelief in any sums of importance.

There is only one thing connected with Belvoir which I do not like—the clock: it goes much too rapidly. At St. Paul's (where it had been my privilege to work in my vocation for some days before I visited Belvoir) the clock was stopped for preparations which were being made to receive the great new bell, and the dean and chapter received an angry letter from an indignant citizen, complaining of the fact, and requesting that men should be employed to move the hands on every minute. I should have liked, on the contrary, to have stopped Time himself at Belvoir, placed the garden roller in front of his scythe, and so prolonged that happy day.

> Linger, I cried, oh radiant Time ! thy power
>   Has nothing more to give ; life is complete ;
> Let but the perfect present, hour by hour,
>   Itself remember, and itself repeat.

* See p. 224.

> But Time pass'd on, in spite of prayer and pleading,
>   Through storm and peril; but that life might gain
> A peace through strife, all other peace exceeding,
>   Fresh joy from sorrow, and new hope from pain.

The last and the happiest of my garden thoughts was this : there is but one Belvoir, but every one who admires those lovely beds and slopes, if he has a plot of ground of his own, however small, may reproduce some of its beauty. With a few large stones, arranged as he sees them there, he may have a miniature rock garden " thick inlaid with patens of bright gold," and silver, and glowing gems, which will most surely repay his loving care with an annual exhibition such as no painter in the world can equal.

ALPINE GARDENS.

IN the last six months I have seen a large number of gardens from one end of the land nigh unto the other, from Cornwall to Yorkshire—gardens magnificent and gardens mean—wild gardens (none so charming as Mr. Boscawen's at Lamorran) and tame gardens; oh, so tame! so scrupulously done to scale and pattern, so shaven and shorn, like the ecclesiastic in the house that Jack built, so raked and rolled, so tied and trim, that they looked more like schools awaiting the government inspector than happy children at play, and only a strong sense of my duty towards my neighbour restrained me from a cheer when I found a sowthistle, and prevented me from brandishing it under his nose. I have seen spring gardens (Belvoir *La Belle, par excellence*) and summer gardens, some laid out with a natural grace, fair and fragrant with hardy shrubs and flowers, annual, biennial, perennial, and some of geometrical design, brilliant with those more tender plants, which cannot abide our frosts, artistic, and attractive, and appropriate, where the site suggests them, as surroundings, for example, to a stately terraced mansion, and where a refined taste selects and groups them.

But, speaking of these gardens generally, I was surprised and disappointed not to find in a large proportion, even where there was evidently no lack of information or of means, those more recent additions to the modes and to the materials of horticulture which have enlarged our happiness and enriched our stores. No gardener, for example, has made experiments, however small, in the formation of a rock garden and the culture of alpine plants without bringing a new gladness to himself and others. Of course, when I speak of a gardener I mean a man who utilizes his eyes and his ears; who in forming a rockery does not set himself to rectify and improve Nature by putting stones on end which she had placed lengthwise; who does not take it for granted that because plants grow out of rocks they have no soil within for their roots; who does not select a clay soil for flowers which repose in sand, nor a shady place for those which only thrive in sunshine; does not set a giant amid dwarfs and allow him to overpower them all (ah me, have I not seen a variegated periwinkle, in cruel alliance with some alpine strawberries, tyrannically appropriating a large space which had once a choice and varied assortment?), but thinks beforehand and watches always. To such a man the introduction of the alpine garden, with its early and exquisite diversities of form and colour, is a new and large delight. It is a new language to a clever linguist, wherein, when he has learned it from A to Z (from anemone to zephyranthes), he finds poetry sublime and sweet. Oh! those welcome, winsome harbingers of spring, those anemones—apennina, blanda, fulgens, Robinsoniana, and the glowing double crimson; those heralds in their beautiful mantles; those cohorts gleaming with purple and gold; those sheets of aubrietia, arabis, iberis; those white and roseate cascades of Phlox Nelsoni and subulata. Oh! those glowing gentians, that lithospermum so intensely, that primula so softly, blue; those auriculas, polyanthuses, oxlips, powdered with gold and silver; that dianthus gleaming in the dull, hard day like the red star of a rocket in the darkness. Oh! those sedums, saxifrages, sempervivums, and other jewels, countless as the harlequin comfits upon a Christmas cake; and yet you rarely find them even where there is the very spot for a rock garden, and stone, and sand, and peat are at hand.

Some seem to think that these plants are delicate as to constitution and difficult as to culture, and that because they are called alpine, they will only flourish on the high places of the earth. Few plants have more vitality, are transferred more successfully, thrive and spread more quickly. There are proofs by the dozen in the rock garden here which were brought by my wife from the mountains of Southern France and Northern Italy, which were many days on their journey hither, sometimes travelling under great disadvantages, at the bottom of luncheon baskets and in other occult localities, lest they should meet the eye of the douanier on the look-out for the phylloxera, but are now as happy in our humble vale as on the banks of the Riviera, or the rocks of the Simplon Pass. I need hardly suggest the inference that, carefully prepared at the nurseries, or given by some friendly neighbour, placed with due regard to site and soil, by those who have seen, heard, or read of the habits of these lovely plants, their success is certain.

And the alpine garden has, in addition, this grand claim upon the admiration of those who study in horticulture, as we should in everything else, the greatest happiness of the greatest number—it may be enjoyed by all. The rich man, if he has the desire and the good taste, may introduce his visitor into a part of his spacious grounds, where in miniature "Hills peep o'er hills, and Alps on Alps arise," where every outline and tint, every form of vegetation, transports them suddenly to Switzerland. And the poor man, with half a dozen big stones, naturally disposed, a few barrows of sandy loam, and a few " bits of things," which he has saved up to buy, or has received from that bounty which, I rejoice to know, is as common as it is honourable with our brothers of the spade, may have a choice little collection of the varied beauty, easily managed, and always interesting.

THE CARNATION.

(Dianthus Coryophyllus.)

WHEN Perdita said,

"The fairest flowers of the season
Are our carnations,"

she was referring to that period of time which intervenes between the first and second efflorescence of the rose, and she was aware, doubtless, that although the object of her delight takes its name from Coronation, it wears a coronet, and not a royal crown. It may be a First Lady in Waiting, and most honourable of all Maids of Honour, but the Queen of all Flowers and Empress of all the Gardens brooks no rival near her throne.

Nevertheless, this dianthus is, as its derivation, διος ανθος, implies, divinely fair, and, always the admiration of gardeners, was never so lovely and never more beloved than now. It is not only the fairest flower of its season, not only like the lady of whom the lover discoursed to the shepherds—

"In form and feature Beauty's Queen,'

but, alike in the secondary as in the primary meaning of the word, "the Pink of Fashion." Over the place where the heart of "the Swell" would be, were it not distributed in small parcels among the belles of the ball, or bestowed in one lot upon "the sweetest girl in England" (how thankful we men ought to be for the replicas of this picture, so exactly copied, that every one is sure that he has the original!), there you see the Carnation! And the wearer walks proudly on, with a swagger, which would be gorgeous, overpowering, were it not toned down by apprehensions of chaff, and jubilant with two blissful delusions —the first that he is "the antlered monarch" of all the deer in the park, and, secondly, that he has secured the finest flower in London—whereas it is made up from *two*.

I cannot say that this "Pink of Fashion" may also be designated as "the mould of form." It is very symmetrical and circular, as you see it on the Exhibition cards, but has become so by adroit manipulation. The petals, by the pincers, have been "long drawn out;" and heartily as I admire and gratefully appreciate the skilful patient art of the florist, and his wonderful success in realizing by selection, inoculation, and hybridizing, his ideals of colour and of shape, I protest against those additions, subtractions, multiplications, and very vulgar fractions, whereby he operates (only too successfully) upon the flower itself.

The carnation is not the only flower which is subject to this exaggeration, *e.g.*, the dahlia and chrysanthemum, but the Royal Rose, I rejoice to know (please, reader, do not ask me *how*), indignantly declines to be "improved," and he who tries to conceal an unsightly "eye" beneath a surreptitious petal, as Miss Squeers essayed to hide her defective organ of vision behind a verandah of drooping curls, or to educe by boisterous breathing a full-blown rose from a bud, will ignominiously fail.

Wherefore, and though I go to the exhibitions of carnations, picotees, and pinks, and gaze admiringly, I have never been desirous to compete, having so many other floral fascinations for the brief leisure at my disposal. The carnation requires the skill of an expert, and the patient devotion of "a man who would sit up all night with a sick cactus," to produce the flowers which take precedence at our shows; and I have known instances in which gardeners themselves have given to their loveliness an undue portion of their time. I remember, for example, walking with my father, who had a great regard for Pomona, and resented any undue intrusions of Flora into his kitchen garden, and how, meeting our gardener between two long rows of carnations, carefully potted, tied to their neat green stakes, and having their big buds bound with bast, he solemnly said, "Evans, if you don't let me have a better supply of fruit and vegetables, I shall probably fancy a carnation tart!" Poor Evans!

" A moment o'er his face a tablet of unutterable thoughts was traced,
And then it faded as it came."

And, as my father afterwards assured me, we had thenceforth more fruit and vegetables.

One more, and yet more striking, instance of attachment to the carnation. "Gentlemen," said my dear old friend, John Keynes, of Salisbury, at a dinner of gardeners and florists, at which I presided many years ago in London, " we are all enthusiastic gardeners, and you will like to hear a marvellous instance of a brother's zeal. I knew an exhibitor of carnations and picotees—Strong was his name, and 'strong' was his affection—who, in stepping out of his cart, at a show held in Winchester, stumbled, fell, and broke his leg. He persisted, nevertheless, in staging his flowers, and remained, with his leg just as it was, until the judges had made their award."

I need hardly say that this strange eventful history was received by the audience with mixed feelings of incredulity and admiration; but when the historian added, as he resumed his seat, "*It was a wooden leg, gentlemen!*" I shall never forget the combination of disgust and delight which was to be seen on the faces of the company.

From romance to reality, *persiflage* to practice. There are three methods of originating carnations, and three modes of outdoor arrangement. They may be raised from seed, from pipings, and from layers, the latter process being far the most reliable, and easily learned from one "object lesson," *i.e.*, from watching any practised operator in the end of July or the beginning of August. The shoots should, in fact, be cut and pegged down as soon as they are ready, for in this, as in all other agricultural and horticultural work, an early start is essential to success—

"Dimidium facti, que bene cepit, habet."

In four or five weeks these scions will be independent of their sires, and in a position to commence business on their own hook, or rather without it, at the beginning of October. They will require water in time of drought.

As to position, here in Rochester, where the dianthus grows wild on the old city walls, and where the light chalky soil and the climate, not far from the sea, seem to be congenial, I grow them (I should say *we* grow them, for my wife bestows most care upon them)—(1) In long beds by themselves, on sunny slopes, with narrow paths, some six feet apart, between them; (2) here and there in our herbaceous border, in clumps of twelve to twenty-four; and (3) in alternate rows with narcissus, so that when the Emperor and the Empress, and Horsfieldii, and Sir Watkin, and Cernuus, *cum multis aliis*, droop and die, they are quickly succeeded by a new and beautiful display.

Are they hardy? The winter, or rather series of winters, which we had in 1890-1, emphatically answer Yes, but I give my plants a coverlet of light manure. The roots may not require the protection, but they like the enrichment of the soil. You do not positively need that eider-down quilt on your bed, but it is an agreeable adjunct when the frozen earth outside puts on its counterpane of snow. Moreover, it pleases me to fancy, and the delusion does no harm, that when I go about my garden, in the winter's cold, my beloved plants look at me from their "top-dressings" with a smile of grateful joy.

In his day, Charles Turner, of Slough, the acknowledged "King of the Florists," was the most successful grower of the carnation, and it was a delectable privilege to go with his Majesty, and his Prime Minister, the Right Honourable John Ball, among his special favourites. Other men of renown have since then achieved greatness—notably, Mr. Dodwell and Mr. Douglas, but Prince Harry, the king's son, still maintains the Royal Supremacy at Slough, and to him I am indebted, as his father's friend, for the following selection of carnations and picotees, as being the best of their kind.

I.

CARNATIONS FOR EXHIBITION.

Scarlet Bizarres.
Admiral Curzon.
Robert Houlgrave.
Robert Lord.

Crimson Bizarres.
Harrison Weir.
Master Fred.
Rifleman.

Pink and Purple Bizarres.
James Taylor.
Sarah Payne.
William Skieving.

Purple Flakes.
Charles Henwood.
Gordon Lewis.
James Douglas.

Scarlet Flakes.
Henry Cannell.
John Ball.
Matador

Rose Flakes.
John Keet.
Sybil.
Thalia.

II.

PICOTEES FOR EXHIBITION.

Red Edged.
Brunette.
John Archer.
John Smith.
Mrs. Gorton.
Princess of Wales.
Thomas William.

Rose and Scarlet Edged
Favorite.
Lady Ponsonby.
Madeline.
Mrs. Harford.
Mrs. Payne.
Mrs. Sharp.

Purple Edged.
Ann Lord.
Baroness Burdett Coutts.
Calypso.
Clara.
Mrs. A. Chancellor.
Tertina.

III.

BORDER CARNATIONS.

Almira.
Amber.
Comtesse de Paris.
Dazzle.
Duchess of Fife.
Hotspur.
Mrs. Apsley Smith.

Mrs. Muir.
Mrs. Reynolds Hole.
Queen of Bedders.
Pride of Penshurst.
Queen of Bedders.
Raby Castle.
Salamanda.

And I would venture to add Germania, which must have been unintentionally omitted, and, as having been beautiful in my own garden, Comte de Chambord and Mary Morris.

IV.

TREE OR PERPETUAL-FLOWERING CARNATIONS.

Amethyst.
Colour Sergeant.
Herald.
Midnight.
Mildred.
Miss Joliffe (improved).
Mrs. Henwood.
Mrs. Lombard.
Mrs. Moore.
Rising Sun.
T. W. Girdlestone.

A WALL OF FLOWERS.

As a background to a long border of herbaceous flowers, some three yards in width and eighty in length, I have planted, against strong, rough hurdles, a variety of climbers, such as Ayrshire, Boursault, Hybrid China, Hybrid Bourbon, Sempervirens, Tea-scented, and a few of the more robust Hybrid Perpetual, Roses, Clematis, Ivies, Honeysuckles, Ceanothus, Indigofera, Hollyhocks, &c; sowing in the spring, on spaces not yet filled up, Canariensis, Convolvulus, Tropœolum, and Sweet Peas. The effect has been already—that is, in the second year—most pleasing, and I contemplate in the following summer a very charming display. The fence is not quite six feet in height, as I had sympathy with the vegetables behind it. I should say that strong posts with wires running through would be available for the same result. The hollyhocks have a stately and attractive beauty at intervals along the line, but they are perishable, and it is well to have a reserve, inexpensive when grown from seed.

TYPES OF GARDENERS.

It has been said to me, " Your love of a garden makes you think all gardeners perfect. The sight of a baize apron through your rose-coloured spectacles is far more beautiful than the velvets of Genoa or Lyons' costliest silk." But I disclaim any such infatuation ; I believe that the gardener has, from his vocation, special advantages to make him genial, intelligent, and high-minded, if he will avail himself of them. That vocation is the oldest, the happiest, the most honourable of all. I was reading the other day in "The English Gardener," a treatise by William Cobbett, late M.P. for Oldham, "of the dispute between the gardeners and the tailors as to the antiquity of their respective callings, the former maintaining that the planting of the garden took place before the sewing of the fig leaves together, and the latter contending that there was no gardening at all till Adam was driven out and compelled to work, but that the sewing was a real and bonâ fide act of tailoring ; " and I was surprised that such a writer on such a subject did not dispose of the question by stating the simple fact that Adam was a gardener from the first, placed in the garden to dress it and to keep it before the Fall, and so instructing us that work in its felicities is the companion of innocence, and only in its miseries the consequence of sin.

Associated by this ancient occupation with all that is brightest and sweetest, all things pleasant to the eye, and good for food; and therefore having, despite the exceptions to which I have referred, communion and co-operation from cultured minds; living in the pure fresh air and sunshine;—the gardener, refined by these influences, is for the most part (I speak from a long and large acquaintance and many a pleasant friendship) of a gentle and thoughtful spirit, having *mens sana in corpore sano*, a tuneful fiddle in a good strong case, a clear conscience and a ruddy cheek; but my admirations are by no means indiscriminate. I suppose that a man may be fond of music without an irrepressible wish to shake hands all round whenever he meets a German band; and while I confidently affirm that the gardener, as a rule, is, from his surroundings, a pleasant and interesting companion, I am painfully aware of many exceptions, of three conspicuously with whom most of my readers have some acquaintance, Messrs. Gawster, Groundsel, and Grunt.

Mr. Gawster has the pride of the peacock without its tail. At least, he has never favoured me with an exposition of plumage which might be termed remarkable. Nevertheless, he assures us that there are no gardens, no houses, no plants, hardy or tender, in Her Majesty's dominions which can vie with his. He does not exhibit because his people do not wish it, and he has quite enough to do at home; tons of fruit, trucks of vegetables, stacks of flowers to be supplied daily. He finds time, notwithstanding, occasionally to attend the shows, and you will hear his voice above all the rest instructing the exhibitors how to grow and train their specialities, assuring them that by carefully obeying his precepts they may realize, as he has realized, such developments of size and beauty as will astonish all who see. If Mr. G. is in business, he walks about his grounds with a demeanour which at once revives our recollection of Alexander Selkirk, and we almost listen for an utterance of the old familiar lines, "I am monarch," &c., &c. If you go into his office, you cannot help reading, as you are intended to read, in huge black letters upon the white page of an open ledger—

THE MARQUIS OF MULIGATAWNEY, K.C.B.,
MULIGATAWNEY CASTLE,
IRELAND;

and you will presently hear Mr. G. inquiring in a loud voice, from one of his men in a distant packing shed, " whether those cases have been sent off to the Duke of Seven Dials, and those cut flowers to Marlborough House."

Mr. Groundsel is head gardener at the Castle of Indolence, on the banks of the river Idle (not the river of that name in Nottinghamshire), and looking down upon Sleepy Hollow. The stream gets as near stagnation as a stream can in the marshy, boggy ground below, and seems to occupy itself more in exhalations, vapours, and fogs than in any right-minded, earnest efforts to go on with its work towards the sea. Higher up there is the same immobility; moss upon wall and walk, upon the glass above and the pots below; enough of the gardener's namesake to make all the canaries of England sing with joy; all the hinges rusty; not a door which does not resent your ingress or egress by a sound of pain; a sense of drowsiness, an exposition of sleep, comes upon you. This land is some hours in advance of that land in which, according to Tennyson, "it seemed always afternoon;" here it seems always bedtime. Mr. Groundsel's appearance invites repose, and suggests armchairs and sofas. He looks like a railway guard going home after extra duty. He reminds us of our brother "poor Pillicoddy, florist and seedsman," struggling against the influence of Poppies, and continually exclaiming, "Rouse me, Sarah!" And yet he is so meek and sleek, inoffensive, comfortable (wants re-potting in fact—I mean re-measuring), so plausible, as he assures you with a yawn, that it is quite impossible to keep such a place in anything like order; that, although you see a lot of lazy fellows loitering about, and helping him to do nothing, you seem to lose any power of protest, and are thankful to escape from the home of the slug and from the voice of the sluggard, lest you should doze into a chronic stupor.

Mr. Grunt seems to be always in that frame of mind which only afflicts ordinary folks when the wind is in the east, when they have been led away by sweets, alcohol, or tobacco, or when their banker takes the liberty of directing their attention to the present state of their account. His life is a prolonged growl. He does a great deal of very good work, but when you praise he snorts at it. If you try to soothe, to ingratiate yourself, by joining in his moans and groans, he will snarl and snap at you like a huge surly retriever of my acquaintance, who, when some young friends of his master returned without their host late from a ball, declined to let them come near the door, and the more they coaxed and addressed him in terms of endearment, "Oh, Tip, you know me, Tip; there's a good Tippy," the more he showed his long white teeth in the moonlight and got himself into position for a spring.

Perhaps there might be fewer examples of these objectionable types if they who have gardens knew more about them, but this is one of those Garden Thoughts which suggests a series.

THE SONG OF THE EXHIBITOR.

Air—"*The Fine Old English Gentleman.*"

Oh, give me air, and syringe me with waters of Cologne !
Dry as a Hortus siccus, run to seed, and overblown,
I try to keep my head up, but down it goes again,
Just like those drooping, stooping flowers, well named the
 sickly men.
    I'm a poor, used-up exhibitor,
    Knocked out of present time.

I've been to all the flower shows, north, south, and east, and
 west,
By rails and roads, with huge van loads of plants I love the
 best ;—
From dusk to dawn, through night to morn, I've dozed 'mid
 clank and din,
And woke, with cramp in both my legs, and bristles on my
 chin.
    I'm a poor, used-up exhibitor,
    Knocked out of present time.

Oh, my orchids look most awk'ardly—stove plants are stoved-in
 quite—
Like my Melon, cut up by the judge, a melancholy sight !

They've broke my Cissus all to bits, as though I had a pair;
And they've brushed in all directions my pretty Maiden's Hair.
    I'm a poor, used-up exhibitor,
    Knocked out of present time.

Look at Erica depressa—depressa, yes, indeed,
As though an alderman sat there, after a heavy feed;
And as for poor Propendens—'tis enough to make one say
Bad words " upon this blasted heath," like Macbeth in the play.
    I'm a poor, used-up exhibitor,
    Knocked out of present time.

There's my Lilium auratum, shrivelled up, and torn, and tanned,—
They may well call it " Japonicum," for it looks as though japanned;
And they've stole my pet new Tricolor, with gold and crimson ribbed;
I meant it for a " *bedder*," but I didn't want it *cribbed*.
    I'm a poor, used-up exhibitor,
    Knocked out of present time.

Here comes my wife! Now, on my life, of Hebes she be queen;
My big prize cup she's filling up with " Bass " of golden sheen—
Delicious! I'm myself once more; and all I want to know,
Is where and when we show again?—hurrah for that next show!
    I'm a fine, revived exhibitor,
    Quite up to present times.

"LOVE AMONG THE TEA ROSES."

THE charming little group so designated was etched for me by my beloved friend, John Leech, and appeared, many years ago, as the frontispiece of *The Gardeners' Annual*. This publication was not exuberantly received by Her Majesty's lieges, and the publishers very generously gave me the plate, having no further use for it.

Its reappearance suggests a few remarks on the most beautiful members of the royal family of the Rose, and, I venture to hope, as the first amateur rosarian who grew tea roses extensively out of doors, that I may claim the privilege of such an utterance.

The best place for them is a border ten feet in width, the longer the better, having an eight feet wall behind, with a southward or eastward aspect. This wall should be covered in due time with Belle Lyonnaise, Cheshunt Hybrid, Gloire de Dijon, L'Idéal, Madame Berard, Maréchal Niel (the best I have grown have been on walls *al fresco*), Rêve d'Or, W. A. Richardson, the Banksians, and Fortune's Yellow.

The best soil is—the best you can get—a rich loam,

a composition of leaf mould and the top spit of pasture, or a good strong clay. I cling most to the latter (and it certainly returns the compliment), because, well dug and hoed, it is most tenacious of manure, and because the roots of the brier stock, on which the tea roses should always be budded, are in the soil which they like the best.

The best sorts (and, in order to be *au courant du jour*, I have obtained from Mr. Prince, of Oxford, who is, I think, *facile princeps* as a grower of tea roses, his selection of the *élite*) are :—

Alba Rosea.	Madame Lambard.
Anna Ollivier.	Marie Van Houtte.
Catharine Mermet.	Miss Ethel Brownlow.
Comtesse Nadaillac.	Mrs. James Wilson.
Ernest Metz.	Niphetos.
Etoile de Lyon.	Perle des Jardins.
Francisca Kruger.	President.
Grace Darling.	Princess of Wales.
Hon. Edith Gifford.	Rubens.
Innocente Pirola.	Souvenir de S. A. Prince.
Jean Ducher.	Souvenir d'un ami.
Madame Cusin.	Souvenir d'Elise Vardon.
Madame Falcot.	Souvenir de Paul Neyron.
Madame C. Kuster.	Sunset.
Madame Hoste.	The Bride.
Madame de Watteville.	

The very *crême de la crême* are Anna Ollivier, Catharine Mermet, Comtesse Nadaillac, Jean Ducher, Marie Van Houtte, and the first three of the four Souvenirs; and, if I might have only one, I should choose Marie Van Houtte. Well grown, it yields the longest and largest abundance of all these border tea roses, and its flowers of pale lemon with a roseate flush are always beautiful.

Plant in November, protect with a thick covering of farmyard manure in December, and prune in April. And if you require more information, write to your bookseller for "A Book about Roses."

www.ingramcontent.com/pod-product-compliance
Lightning Source LLC
Chambersburg PA
CBHW032132230426
43672CB00011B/2309